To Billie —
Enjoy the book —

THE CBS MURDERS

Some day a Movie?
Never a Play !!!

John Wa~

BOOKS BY RICHARD HAMMER

The CBS Murders
The Vatican Connection
Mr. Jacobson's War (novel)
An End to Summer (novel)
Hoodlum Empire
Gangland, U.S.A.
The Illustrated History of Organized Crime
The Last Testament of Lucky Luciano (with Martin A. Gosch)
The Court-Martial of Lt. Calley
One Morning in the War
Between Life and Death

THE CBS MURDERS

Richard Hammer

William Morrow and Company, Inc.
New York

Library of Congress Cataloging-in-Publication Data

Hammer, Richard, 1928–
  The CBS murders.
  1. Murder—New York (N.Y.)—Case studies.   I. Wales, John Richard.   II. Title.
HV6534.N5H35   1987   364.1′523′097471   86-31288
ISBN 0-688-06609-7

Printed in the United States of America

First Edition

1 2 3 4 5 6 7 8 9 10

BOOK DESIGN BY OKSANA KUSHNIR

For
Jerome Perles

Acknowledgments

This book could not have been written without the cooperation and assistance of members of the New York City Police Department who were directly involved in the investigation of what became known as the CBS murders, nor without access to certain files, documents, memoranda, and records of the Federal Bureau of Investigation relating to its probe of the swindle that led to those murders.

Most particularly, I would like to express my gratitude for their patience and help to the members of the task force charged with uncovering the crime, Detectives Richard Chartrand and Robert Patterson of the Midtown North precinct and to Lieutenant Richard Gallagher and Detective John Wales, both now retired from the force.

—R.H.

THE CBS
MURDERS

PART
ONE

MURDER

1

April 12, 1982
Easter Monday. An ordinary day in Manhattan. The sudden, unexpected spring blizzard that had howled across the city the previous week, leaving in its wake more than a foot of snow and a paralyzed metropolis, was now no more than an unpleasant memory. A few days of warm sun and temperatures well up into the fifties had turned the pristine mountainous drifts into shrinking mounds of gray slush and then into raging rivers of filthy water. With the start of the new workweek and continued bright weather, the rivers had dried and vanished, and the city was warm and pleasant with spring.

In Midtown North, as in other police precincts, it was business as usual this day after the holiday. A polyglot precinct is Midtown North, microcosm of the public picture of New York. It stretches from the Hudson River piers and the decrepit West Side Highway east to the soaring towers and exclusive shops that line Fifth Avenue, from just above the sleaze of Times

15

Square north to the fringes of the glittering mecca of culture in Lincoln Center. Within these boundaries lies the communications capital of North America, the editorial offices and the headquarters of the television network giants, where the decisions are made about what Americans will read and watch. The tastes, trends, and desires of America—indeed, of much of the world—in a hundred different areas are debated and dictated in the skyscraper offices of the multinational corporations that compete for air and ground space along the canyonlike avenues. Through a hundred small, dingy yet impregnably armored offices along one short block of West Forty-seventh Street pass enough gold and diamonds every day to make an ancient Indian mogul feel deprived and to bring delight and riches to the South African mine owners.

That is one face of Midtown North. There is another, a dozen others. For every steel and glass tower there are twenty shabby, ill-repaired lofts housing hundreds of small businesses just barely keeping afloat. For every department store and specialty shop, there are fifty hole-in-the-wall cigar stores, pawnshops, bookie joints, and seedy discount outlets peddling merchandise that seems to evaporate into dust on first use. For every luxury hotel luring out-of-town tourists and business conventions, there are a dozen flophouses and welfare shelters. For every cooperative and condominium and high-priced rental apartment catering to the rich, there are a hundred tenements. For every first-run cinema palace there are five porno movie houses, peep shows, and live-sex-act establishments. For every successful businessman, there are ten shady operators skirting the edges of legitimacy, often with an outward face of respectability. For every tourist and honest citizen wandering through the area or working in it, there is a pimp and his hookers, a pusher and his junkies, to say nothing of the thieves, petty and grand, the hoodlums, organized and unorganized, and all the rest.

That is the surface. But beneath the wealth, glitter, and success, beneath the contrasting poverty, bleakness, and failure, there is a barely concealed stench of desperation and fear. There

16

is the fear of failure, the fear of competition, the fear of strangers, the fear of friends who may not be friends, the fear in the streets, and the fear of the streets. "The mass of men," Thoreau wrote, "lead lives of quiet desperation." It is true here as everywhere. But, for some, their fears drive them away from the quiet hopelessness to desperate acts.

In the heart of the area, on West Fifty-fourth Street between Eighth and Ninth avenues, stands the forbidding fortress that is Midtown North. Though they are often cynical, talk about their work as just a job, and gripe about the long hours and lousy pay, the men who spread a thin blue shield from this drab building think of themselves as the soldiers of the city, the area's protection, only protection, when desperation becomes overt. Their struggle is unending, and days blend into days, leaving little to mark them from the ones that have gone before.

On this Monday after Easter, they had gone about their work just about as always. There had been only the usual burglaries and robberies, muggings and purse snatchings, rapes and assaults, family arguments and traffic accidents, nothing unusual, nothing to make this day remain fixed in the memory.

What there had not been was a murder. Nobody doubted that there would be one, if not that day, then soon. In Manhattan, where murder is committed on the average of more than ten times a week, Midtown North sees more than its share. Still, that Monday had passed without one and the day was ending, twilight descending over the city, the lights beginning to go on, the stores and offices closing, the commuters from the suburbs and the city's residential areas beginning the long trek homeward.

By six o'clock, halfway through their eight-hour shift, the detectives up in the second-floor squad room had little enough to do but sit around and argue over who would catch the next murder when it happened, as surely it would, supposing it happened during their shift. It was not a job anyone particularly looked forward to. It would mean, if the usual pattern was followed, going out to some rundown tenement where a family quarrel had turned violent, or to some small store whose owner lay in a pool of blood after resisting a robbery, or to some mean street where a mugging had ended in death. It would mean long, endless hours without sleep. And then, no matter how often they had been seen, a dead body, a murder victim, was not a pleasant sight, not something anyone ever completely got used to.

In the room then were six men: Richard Chartrand, John Johnston, Jack Hart, Stanley Shapiro, Robert Patterson, and Jack Duffy.

Richie Chartrand was the oldest and most experienced. He had been a cop for nearly thirty years, a detective for most of that time, in the old homicide bureau for years until the bureau was disbanded and its experts dispersed to precincts around the city. He was a soft-spoken man who appeared, on the surface, mild-mannered and colorless. But he had an incisive and intuitive mind that could cut through obfuscations to the core, and in that muted voice there was often an edge of cynicism and a sardonic wit. Dressed always with neatness and precision, in a suit and tie and, when outdoors, a hat, he looked more like a businessman, or, somebody said, an FBI supervisor, than a cop. He had seen enough murders to last a dozen lifetimes and invariably was the man turned to in times of crisis.

Bobby Patterson was the newest and youngest man on the team. He had been a cop for about fifteen years, since the day he turned twenty-one, and a detective for the past two. Despite an attempt to look older and tougher by growing a moustache, he still gave the appearance of a raw, untried rookie. In the previous six weeks he had handled two murder cases, including the last one to come through the office.

If and when a murder came, everyone agreed, it was Stanley Shapiro's turn to catch it. He hadn't had one in as long as anyone could remember. He was a good cop, a capable detective, but the ideal role for him, he devoutly believed, was second man and not the leader in an investigation, and he had no desire to be out front if something happened that night.

But nothing had happened, and the argument was only

desultory and academic. "What the hell," Patterson said at one point, "I don't care. I can use the overtime."

"It's Stanley's turn," the others argued. "A call comes, Stanley catches it."

Shapiro didn't like that idea at all.

The argument meandered. It could have been settled before it even started if Lieutenant Richard Gallagher, the man in charge of the squad, had been there, but Dick Gallagher was taking the day off, was at home in Rockland County attending to some early spring gardening.

And then the phone rang. Patterson was closest. He picked it up, listened, made some notes. Around him, the argument went on. Patterson hung up, turned to the others. "We'd better settle this right now," he said. "We've got three dead bodies over on Pier Ninety-two."

Chartrand looked at him. "Is that some kind of joke, Bobby?" he asked.

"No joke," Patterson said. "That was the uniform. We've got three dead ones on the pier."

"Get a confirmation," Chartrand ordered.

Patterson returned to the phone.

Shapiro rushed for another phone. "Jesus," he said, "I'd better get hold of the lieutenant."

Jack Duffy, the clerk in the squad room, beat him to the phone, was already dialing Gallagher's number.

"Stanley," somebody said, "you're up."

Shapiro shook his head. He would, he said, wait for orders from Gallagher.

Chartrand sighed. "What the hell," he said, "we'll take one apiece. Bobby, you had the last one, so you stick around and handle the phones, make all the notifications and the rest of the crap." He turned to John Johnston and Jack Hart. "Us three," he said, "let's go."

19

2

A half hour earlier, two blocks north and three west, the S.S. *Rotterdam* was just leaving its Hudson River berth at Pier Ninety-two for a week-long Caribbean cruise. Two of the three adjacent piertop parking lots, each about the size of a football field, were emptying out, the visitors who had come to see their friends and relatives off driving slowly down the off ramp, stopping at the gatehouse at the exit to pay the parking fee and then continuing on into the city traffic. In the third, northernmost of the lots, there still were thirty or more cars. But this lot was reserved mainly for long-term parkers who paid $40 a month for the privilege, and it still would be a little time before most of them left work in nearby offices, shops, and factories and retrieved their cars for the ride home.

A silvery 1980 Chevrolet van turned off the roadway under the West Side Highway and started to move along the up ramp toward the parking area, toward the long-term lot. The driver of the van was a burly, bullet-headed man in his late forties with a drooping, nearly blind right eye, the result of a childhood accident. He wore a light-colored windbreaker. He chewed idly on a matchstick. Stopping momentarily at the mechanical gate, he pulled a ticket from the slot, waited for the arm to rise, and then drove through and up the ramp. He passed the first and second lots and then turned into the third, the long-term lot.

His name was Donald Nash; he had been born Donald Bowers but had adopted his mother's maiden name, according to stories around the West Side docks where he was long a familiar figure, at the insistence of his relatives, the overlords of the International Longshoremen's Union's "Pistol" Local 824 during its heyday, who considered him unworthy of bearing the same last name.

He drove slowly through the lot. He knew precisely where he was going and what he was going to do, what he had been hired and paid to do. He had thought about it and planned it meticulously for a long time. If all went as he had worked it out in his mind—and he knew no reason why it wouldn't, for he had been in that lot, a long-term parker himself, often enough over the past week to know when people came and left and where they parked their cars—then he would have done what he had come to do and departed within the next thirty minutes. And after that, if anybody looked for him—and there was no reason why they should—he would be where anybody could find him and nobody would ever think of looking. He would be serving a twenty-day sentence in the Manhattan Correctional Center.

About halfway down the lot, he spotted what he was looking for, a 1980 Blue BMW 320i. He slowed, started to turn in next to it, on the driver's side. And then he was faced with the first unexpected hitch in his carefully conceived plan. Nearly every day for the past week, he had been in and out of that lot, morning and evening, observing the regularity with which people arrived and departed, noting that most invariably left their cars in precisely the same location every day. He had been counting on those inbred patterns. But now, for the first time, the spot on the left side of the BMW was taken. He stopped the van, considered, made his decision, threw the gears into reverse, backed a little, and then turned head on into the spot on the right, the passenger side of the BMW; it was, at least, still unoccupied. He might have made things a little easier for himself had he backed in, but every other car on the lot was parked head in, and his van, the only one on a lot filled with sedans, was conspicuous enough as it was without making it stand out even more by parking the wrong way.

He turned off the engine, got out, walked around to the driver's side of the BMW. Taking the matchstick from his mouth, he jammed the matchstick tightly and deeply into the lock, far enough in so it could neither be seen nor easily removed. He returned to the van.

While he waited, he finished his preparations. He made certain the sliding panel door on the right side of the van was unlocked and slid open easily. Within the protection of the driver's seat, he removed a .22-caliber automatic from its hiding place, removed a silencer from his pocket, and fitted the pieces together. He loaded the automatic, then placed it on the seat next to him. He settled back. He knew he did not have long to wait.

Two blocks south, on West Fifty-fourth Street just in from Twelfth Avenue, thirty-seven-year-old Margaret Barbera, an attractive, dark-haired woman with strikingly large dark eyes, was closing her desk, saying good night, and starting out the door of the Camera Service Center. For just a week, she had been the company's bookkeeper. Nobody in the firm knew much about her, though. She kept to herself, had lunch alone, arrived in the morning and left in the evening right on time, and revealed nothing about her personal life. But, then, she had never been one to open herself to strangers, and she had few friends. Ruth Clapp, the office manager who had interviewed and hired her three weeks earlier, would say later that Barbera had answered an ad in *The New York Times* for a bookkeeper, and though nobody had yet had time to check out her references, they had appeared on the surface to be more than adequate, and she had demonstrated in her week of employment that she had known how to deal with figures and account books. About the only other thing that Mrs. Clapp knew was that Barbera had asked for a delay of a couple of weeks before she started the job. She had had some trouble with her last employer, she explained, not going into what kind of trouble, and probably would have to appear as a witness against him in some pending court case, and further, she wanted time to clean up work she was doing for her own personal clients. Her request had been granted, and she had begun work on Monday, April 5.

If Barbera was worried or if she had any premonitions of danger as she walked out the doorway that night, she kept them to herself. The last sight anyone in the camera shop had of her was as she passed through the doorway and turned west, heading for the parking lot at Pier Ninety-two, where she had reserved a monthly space the previous week, to retrieve her BMW and drive home to her apartment in Queens.

At almost the same moment, three blocks north on West Fifty-seventh Street, Leo Kuranuki, Robert Schulze, and Edward Benford were just leaving their jobs at the CBS studios in the middle of the block between Tenth and Eleventh avenues and heading for their cars at Pier Ninety-two. All three were in their fifties and all were veteran employees of the network, Kuranuki as a studio maintenance manager, Schulze as manager of videotape maintenance, and Benford as a broadcast technician. Both Kuranuki and Schulze were bachelors and sedentary men, somewhat overweight and out of shape. Benford, married and with an eighteen-year-old son in college, was a skier, hiker, and golfer in his spare time, though his activities had been somewhat curtailed after a heart bypass operation a couple of years before.

They had just about reached the ramp to the parking lot when another CBS employee, Angelo Sicca, who worked in the construction shop and knew Schulze well, came around the corner about fifty yards behind them, saw them, and called out for them to wait up for him. Apparently they didn't hear his shout and continued up the ramp, Sicca following at a distance.

* * *

Margaret Barbera reached the piertop parking lot first, walked through it toward her car, went around to the driver's side, fished in her purse for the key, removed it, and tried to insert it into the lock. It wouldn't go. The lock was jammed. She went around to the other side, the passenger side, and started to put the key in the lock.

Nash was watching from inside the van. He was ready. As Barbera stood beside her car, Nash, holding his .22 automatic in one hand, leaned out the window of the van, placed the pistol against the back of her head, and fired one shot. Barbera was dead before she hit the pavement.

Kuranuki, Schulze, and Benford were well into the lot, heading for their cars. They stopped suddenly and turned. Sicca, too, was in the lot, approaching his own car. He heard a soft pop. He turned to look in the direction of the sound. He saw Barbera slumping to the ground, saw Nash getting out of the van, bending over her, beginning to drag her around the front of the van, onto the ledge that borders the area, and disappearing. He could see nothing else, but he heard what he recognized from his own long experience with vans as the sound of the sliding door in the side opening, heard a hollow thud, heard the door slide shut.

Sicca unlocked his own car and started to get inside. He glanced around and saw Kuranuki leave Schulze and Benford and move toward the van, concern on his face. Kuranuki disappeared around the side of the van but Sicca heard his voice, asking, "What's going on?"

Nash saw him, stopped, stared at him. "You didn't see nothin', did you?" he demanded. And then, not waiting for a response, he raised the pistol, brought it within inches of Kuranuki's head, and fired. Sicca heard another soft pop. Kuranuki was dead.

Ten or fifteen feet away, Schulze and Benford saw it all with disbelief, hardly comprehending yet what they had stumbled into, what they had just witnessed. They turned and started to move quickly away. Sicca saw them, didn't realize that they were in a panic, were beginning to flee for their lives. He thought they were just going to their cars and Kuranuki would be appearing from around the van any second. "I thought that was the end of it," he said.

It was not. Nash suddenly appeared around the side of the van. In his hand he was holding the long-barreled pistol, the .22 with its silencer attached. Schulze began to run. Nash caught up with him in seconds, after a chase of no more than a few yards, grabbed his arm, brought the pistol up to Schulze's right ear, snapped, "You didn't see nothin'," and then fired. Sicca heard another soft pop. Schulze fell to the pavement, dead.

Nash started after Benford. But Sicca was sure that before that chase began, Nash had looked in his direction. "I had the feeling he was looking at me." Terrified, Sicca climbed into his car, huddled low behind the wheel so as not to be seen, afraid to look and perhaps make eye contact with the killer. He started the engine, put the car in reverse, and began to back out of his spot. But his eyes were drawn back to the scene, unwillingly. Nash was chasing Benford, who was running toward the end of the pier. Nash caught up with him, grabbed Benford by the arm. Benford tried to break loose. Nash raised the pistol, fired into Benford's head. There was another soft pop. Benford fell. He, too, was dead.

Nash turned back toward the van.

Sicca raced his engine, backed out, drove as fast as he could toward the exit ramp and down it. As he reached the gatehouse at the bottom, he glanced in the rearview mirror. Terror swept through him. The van was behind him, separated by only one other car. He was certain the killer must have seen him on the pier and so must be after him. All Sicca wanted was to get away as fast as he could. He reached the gatehouse at the bottom of the ramp. Normally, when only long-term parkers are in the lot, the gatehouse would be closed and empty. But this had been a ship day and so the attendant was still on duty to collect parking fees from anyone who might have lingered after the *Rotterdam* sailed. Sicca thrust his ticket into the hands of the attendant, William Streiter, and in a panic, shouted, "The guy in the van behind me! He just hit three people up on the pier!" Then he was out and onto the street, heading north and praying.

In his booth, Streiter stared after Sicca in bewilderment. The van went by, not bothering to pause even to hand over the parking ticket. Streiter shrugged. He figured that what Sicca meant by his words was that there had been a minor traffic accident up on the pier, that the van had crashed into a couple of cars. He picked up the phone in the booth to call security, to ask a guard to go up to the pier to see what kind of damage had been done. There was no answer. He kept trying.

Out on Twelfth Avenue, Sicca was racing north. His eyes were pinned hypnotically to his rearview mirror, watching. He caught sight of the silver van emerging from the ramp, watched as it turned south on the avenue. He took a deep breath. Maybe the killer hadn't seen him after all. He made a U-turn and headed back to the pier, drove up the ramp and out onto the scene of the massacre.

As he got out of his car, Sicca noticed that another CBS technician, Robert Schlop, a film and videotape editor, was part-way along the pier, halted, staring at Kuranuki's body, which sprawled on the ground ahead of him. Sicca and Schlop saw each other. "Hey," Schlop shouted, "I think this guy's hurt! You'd better call an ambulance!"

"The police," Sicca said. "I think he's dead. And if you go on down the pier, you're going to find two more."

Schlop stared at Sicca for a moment. Sicca turned quickly away, racing for the phone. He called police emergency, 911, and gasped out the news of the murders. Schlop followed a little behind, heading for another phone. He called CBS, asked for the news department, shouted the news, and told the news editor he'd better send a camera crew to the pier right away.

3

It took Chartrand, with Johnston and Hart, only a few minutes to reach the pier from Fifty-fourth Street. But by the time they got there, it was, Chartrand remembers, "chaos." There were uniformed cops everywhere and more arriving every minute. There were television camera crews and newspapermen. Though it had gotten the call from its own man, CBS was beaten to the scene, and to the air, by New York's independent stations, whose mobile news units, cruising as always through the city, their radios tuned to police frequencies, picked up the first alerts to go out from the 911 operator and raced to the scene.

Within the next hour, nearly all the ranking brass from the city's police department were on the pier, along with most of the city's high elected officials. "Everybody was there," Chartrand says. "The commissioner, the chief of detectives, everybody. I think even some son-of-a-bitch from Teaneck, New Jersey, showed up with scrambled eggs all over his cap. Guys from the Port Authority police. I never knew until then that they had guys with stars. Theoretically, the piers were under their jurisdiction, and we stayed away unless they invited us in or unless there was a serious crime, like auto theft or murder. Of course, this was a serious crime, so we settled the matter of jurisdiction right then."

Lieutenant Dick Gallagher had received the call at home, had received a second call a few minutes later as he was heading for his car, that call filling him in on what sketchy details were available. He raced across the George Washington Bridge and down the Henry Hudson Parkway, wondering all the time what was going to greet him when he reached Pier Ninety-two. "They told me," he remembers, "that the three dead guys were from CBS. They didn't know much more than that. And all I could think was, Jesus, have we got some kind of violent network feud on our hands." He wasn't the only one to have that thought at this stage; it occurred to almost everyone else, and if it were so, the implications were appalling.

But Gallagher and the high brass still were on their way, their speculations only that, when Chartrand reached the pier less than fifteen minutes after the first shot had been fired. He took one look at the chaos, at the growing mob scene that could have been out of some Hogarthian nightmare, at what appeared to be the lack of any organized control. He immediately stepped in and took charge. He could see the bodies of Kuranuki, Schulze, and Benford where they had fallen, lying in pools of blood around their heads, untouched yet except for a cursory examination to confirm that they were dead. Neither the medical examiner nor the police photographers had arrived, and nobody was about to disturb anything until they had. It was almost impossible, with all the people milling about and more arriving every minute, to see much more than that. Chartrand could not rid his mind of the thought that maybe there still were more bodies farther out on the pier or concealed behind some of the parked cars.

He did what had to be done. He ordered the area cleared, moving the television crews and the newsmen away from the scene and holding them at bay off to one side; maybe they could

28

see something from there and maybe they couldn't; he didn't care, as long as they stayed out of his way.

Sicca and Schlop were brought over and introduced to him, along with Streiter, who had been summoned from his parking booth at the bottom of the ramp. Chartrand exchanged a few words with them, just enough to hear about the van and the driver who had carried a long-barreled pistol and had shot Kuranuki, Schulze, and Benford. An alarm went out for a light-colored van, which was all anybody knew at that moment. Whatever else Sicca particularly, and Schlop and Streiter had to say could wait for later; there were things that Chartrand had to do first before he could pay much attention to their stories, before he could question them in full. They were handed over to other cops, separated so that when he finally did hear them their stories still would be fresh, they would not have had an opportunity to compare notes and, perhaps, try to resolve discrepancies, if there were any. They were isolated and kept waiting until he had time for them.

He turned to the bodies then. And as he did, both the medical examiner and the police photographer arrived. "The bodies had not been searched until then," Chartrand says. "So while we did the photographs and before the medical examiner went to work, we did the search of the bodies and the immediate areas around them, and each search was done by a uniformed officer in my presence, so that I would know what was found. The reason it was done that way was because I wanted it done that way, because normally you try to assume that whatever case you go out on, you're going to wind up with. So if you treat them all like your own from the beginning, you can do a better job." Chartrand's assumption was, of course, correct. It was his case from the start.

Slowly and carefully they went over the bodies and, inch by inch, over the pier, now illuminated by blinding portable lights brought in by the police. Three shell casings were discovered, one near each body. And near Kuranuki's body they came upon a pair of woman's shoes, a plastic hairband and an open purse, some coins, car keys, and other things scattered around it. An examination of the keys showed they belonged to a BMW, and there was a BMW only a few feet away.

Chartrand took the keys. "I did what every normal person does," he says. "I tried to open the car from the driver's side. And I couldn't get it open. So we had to open it from the passenger side." (The next day, a police locksmith pulled the lock from the driver's side of the BMW and found a sliver of wood, a piece of a matchstick, jammed well up into it.)

If neither Chartrand nor anyone else had any idea where or how the BMW, the purse, and the shoes fitted into the carnage that had taken place on the pier, still, naturally enough, their attention increasingly focused on the car. But those thirty-odd other cars on the pier, some of whose owners were now appearing to claim them and drive home after work, could not be ignored, either. There was no telling if one or more of them might be a piece of the puzzle as well. "We began a check of every vehicle on the pier," Chartrand says. "Who they belonged to, what they were doing up there, everything. Some of them belonged to long-term parkers, some to people who had left them while they went on the cruise. It took a long time. Many of the people who were coming up to get their vehicles that night were denied their vehicles. They couldn't get them. It was an inconvenience, of course, but a necessary one."

It was, though, that $20,000 German car that really intrigued them. The conviction that it must be central began to grow. In his initial brief exchange with Sicca, Chartrand had been told of the woman being dragged around the van, and the van had been parked alongside the BMW. Who was the woman? The car had New Jersey license plates, and the registration in the glove compartment listed it as belonging to a Margaret Barbera of 631 Cumberland Road in Teaneck, N.J. The driver's license and other identification found in the purse, and the application filled out with Kinney System, Inc., operator of the pier parking lot and dozens more around the city, were all in the name of Margaret Barbera of 613 Grandview Avenue in the Ridgewood section of Queens. That discrepancy caused hardly a lifted eyebrow. It is not an unknown practice for some

30

New Yorkers to register their cars in New Jersey or Connecticut, where insurance rates are a lot lower or where, if they are deeply in debt, the car can be protected from the claims of New York creditors.

Still, it did present a minor problem. "There was as a result," Chartrand notes, "a little difficulty in establishing if this is the person who is gone." There was no Margaret Barbera listed in the Teaneck phone book, but there was a Queens telephone number as well as the Queens address on the application she had filed with Kinney, and it matched the Queens number found on various items in the purse. Over the next hours, the number was called several times. There was never an answer.

In that purse, too, the police found Camera Service Center identification. Detectives were sent to the shop on West Fifty-fourth Street. They were told that, indeed, Margaret Barbera worked there, had worked there for just a week. And she had left work just before six. She must have been going to the parking lot on Pier Ninety-two because she had told people that she had rented a spot there for her car.

It was time to talk to the witnesses. Over the next hours and all through the night, Chartrand and others went through their stories, concentrating especially on Sicca, since he was the only actual witness to the shootings. He was questioned three times that night: a brief interrogation on the pier while Chartrand was busy with the bodies and the search of the crime scene; a second, lengthier conversation on the pier by Chartrand after he had completed that search; and a long session, lasting several hours, back at Midtown North. Sicca, Chartrand says, "was very astute. He was not the type of person who could be swayed or influenced. He laid it out for us. He told us what he saw and what he didn't see. And he was very, very accurate. His description of the killer wasn't very good because he never got a really good look. He was deathly afraid for his own life. He was afraid that his presence on the pier at that time had been detected by the shooter, and he was trying to look to see what was going on and still trying to remain unseen. And when

31

he drove off the pier and looked in his rearview mirror and here's the van right behind him, one car away, he was petrified. He was terrified that he was going to be taken. There's no question that anyone who confronted the shooter while he was fleeing was going to die, or that he was going to make every effort to see that he died."

At the end of those first hours in the evening of April 12, then, the police were faced with a massive and grisly puzzle and they had only a few pieces, not nearly enough yet to make much sense of it, hardly enough even to begin to put the first pieces together. They had the bodies of Leo Kuranuki, Robert Schulze, and Edward Benford, all run down in that Pier Ninety-two parking lot and killed by single shots from a .22-caliber automatic. They were convinced that there had been a silencer attached to the pistol; the soft pops heard by the only witness, Angelo Sicca, indicated that. They had the shell casings from the pistol, casings found near the bodies. They had Sicca's story that a woman, perhaps shot and killed, had been abducted and thrown into a white or silver van. The indications were that the woman's name was Margaret Barbera; she was the owner of a BMW that had been parked next to the van, and it appeared to have been abandoned; its driver's door lock had been jammed; her purse and, perhaps, her shoes were lying near Kuranuki's body and the BMW. At this point, nobody had the slightest idea why she had been marked as the killer's intended victim, if, indeed, that was what she was. It could have been, for all they knew, the violent end to a lovers' quarrel, or she might have been the victim of a hired assassin; nobody could be sure of anything. They knew that the killer had escaped in a light-colored van and had headed south once he was out of the parking-lot ramp. They had, from Sicca, a sketchy description of him as a tall, slim man somewhere between thirty and forty, but Sicca had said that description was only a guess, that the light was dim, that he was making every effort to hide from the killer's gaze and so never really got a good look. He was just making a guess, but he could be completely wrong about it.

It was not much to go on. But there was a need to move

rapidly. They were faced, even in those first hours, with a public outcry, and it would swell in volume as the days passed. This was the worst case of multiple homicides, aside from the internecine killings in the underworld, that the city had seen in years. The victims were three innocent, respectable men, bystanders, who had sought only to come to the aid of somebody in possible distress, and their reward had been death. The fact that they were employees of one of the most powerful organs of communications in the land, CBS, made the pressure for a quick solution even greater. CBS was not only playing the story for all it was worth in news value, as were all the other television stations and the newspapers, but also the network was offering a $25,000 reward for information leading to the arrest and conviction of the killer. The case thus became top priority for the police.

4

Had Donald Nash kept his head, there might have been no slaughter on Pier Ninety-two that April evening. There would have been only a single murder, the one he had been hired to commit. And the chances are, he would have gotten away with it. When Leo Kuranuki approached with his question, "What's going on?" if Nash had replied, "It's nothing. My wife and I were having a little argument, that's all. It's all over now. Thanks anyway," Kuranuki probably would have turned away, and that would have been that.

But Nash lost his cool. He had been edgy ever since reaching the pier. First, there was the very fact of the murder he was about to commit and the wait for his victim to arrive. And then there was the hitch in his plan, that car parked on the left side of the BMW, the spot he had meant to be his. If he had been able to park there, the van's sliding door would have been directly opposite the driver's door of the BMW. It would have been a simple matter to lean out and shoot Margaret Barbera while she was unlocking her car, then haul her into the van through the open sliding door without ever having to leave the shelter of the van's interior, then slide the door shut. It would have been over in an instant. Nobody would have seen anything, and the most anybody could have heard was the soft pop of the silencer-equipped automatic, a sound that would have made hardly an impression on that vast pier. But that other car was there. He had been forced to park on the passenger side of Barbera's car and then, once he had shot her, drag her around the van. That had put him in the open, naked to any eyes during those critical moments. Kuranuki, Schulze, and Benford had seen him then. Kuranuki had approached with his question. Nash was sure he had no other choice but to kill the three witnesses.

In panic, he sped off the pier. Sicca had nothing to worry about. With his limited vision and his preoccupation with too many other things, he had not noticed Sicca, and so the car up ahead meant nothing. Nash wanted only to flee from that place as fast as he could. He raced by the gatehouse, past Streiter, not bothering to slow and hand in his parking ticket. Streiter paid him no attention. He was turning over in his mind what Sicca had said about somebody hitting three people up on the pier, was reaching for the phone to call security and ask them to check on it.

Once out on Twelfth Avenue and heading south, Nash forced himself to slow, to keep within the speed limit, to obey the red lights. The last thing he needed at that moment, with Barbera's body in the back of the van, was to be picked up for breaking a traffic law. He needed time to consider what course to follow now. His original plan, to kill Barbera undetected and then drive her through the Lincoln Tunnel and dispose of her body where it would never be found in the New Jersey swamps, was impossible now, he was convinced. The alarm must be out, and the exits from the tunnel blocked, cars and vans being checked. (He was wrong, as it turned out. That alarm still was some time in the future, and he could have gone through the tunnel and emerged safe. But there was no way he could have

known that.) He had to come up with an alternative. He drove
south along the avenue as far as Forty-fourth Street, turned
east there for two blocks, turned north on Tenth Avenue, drove
a block, and then turned west on Forty-fifth Street. He stopped
halfway down the block, parking at the curb in front of number
436. It had taken him, even with all his extra care and caution,
less than eight minutes to reach his destination from the pier.

The building on West Forty-fifth Street was home to Vinny
Russo catering, purveyor of breakfasts and lunches to the movies and television shows being filmed on location in the city.
Like many longtime businessmen and inhabitants along the
West Side docks, Russo had known Nash for years and had a
certain tolerant fondness for him. Some months earlier, when
Nash had mentioned that he was setting up a small electrical
contracting business and needed some desk space to operate
out of, Russo had told him, sure, he could put a desk and a
telephone in a back corner of Russo's shop. Nash had taken
possession, installed the telephone and an answering machine,
and every few days, when he was in Manhattan, he would stop
by to pick up his messages, what few there ever were. The shop
normally was closed well before six in the evening and, Russo
later insisted, Nash did not have a key, he had never given him
one nor permitted him to have one. That day, though, there
was no need for a key.

Leaving the van, and Barbera's body in the back, out at the
curb, Nash rushed to the door of Russo's shop. It was unlocked
and open. There had been a major water leak within the past
hours, and the building's superintendent, Alberto Torres, was
inside, finishing the repairs, cleaning and mopping up. He and
Nash had been friends for years. When he saw Nash, though,
he was surprised not just at his appearance at this unexpected
hour but also at his condition. Nash was in extreme distress;
he was shaking, out of breath, and drenched with sweat; he
looked as though he had just come out of a shower or a steam
bath. Nash barely greeted Torres. He made straight for his
desk, picked up the phone, and dialed a number in Keansburg,
N.J., the home of his twenty-nine-year old nephew, Thomas

36

Dane. Nash knew that if there was one person in the world he could depend on in time of need, it was Dane. Dane idolized him, looked on him not just as an uncle but also as his best friend, a father. There was nothing Dane would not do for him.

The line was busy.

Nash hung up, dialed again, this time his own number in Keansburg. His common-law wife of seventeen years, Jean Marie, answered. He told her he was trying to reach Dane, it was urgent that he talk to him, but the line was busy. He told her to walk the two and a half blocks to Dane's house, tell him to get off the phone because Nash was trying to get through. She did as she was told.

Dane was talking to his girlfriend in Manhattan, had been talking to her for about ten minutes, when Jean Marie Nash rang the doorbell and gave him Nash's message. Dane went back to the phone and told his girlfriend, "I'm sorry. My uncle is trying to reach me. I have to hang up. But I'll call you back after I talk to him."

On Forty-fifth Street, Nash waiting nervously and impatiently, counting the minutes he knew it would take his wife to reach Dane. Outside, he could hear the shattering screams of the sirens as police car after police car raced north to Pier Ninety-two.

When he figured enough time had passed, he dialed Dane again and this time got through. He told Dane it was vital that they meet. He was in Manhattan and would be heading for New Jersey within a few minutes. Dane should meet him just off the parkway on the way to Keansburg, a spot where they had met several times before. Dane agreed and hung up. He called his girlfriend back and told her, "That was my uncle. I have to meet him later on." Then, for the next eight minutes, he conversed with her, picking up where they had left off.

For some moments after his call was completed, Nash sat silently at his desk, holding his head in his hands. Suddenly he looked up at Torres. "Alberto," he said, "my God, I just shot three people. They're all dead. You have the keys to the fence of the parking lot next door. Can I put the van in there?"

Torres was stunned, unbelieving, appalled. He stared at Nash. What he didn't know was that there was a body in the back of the van. Nash didn't tell him that. He shook his head. He wanted no part of this, did not want to become involved in any way. "I can't do it," he said. "The people who rent the lot, they come in very early in the morning, and if anybody's parked there but them, I'll lose my job."

Nash just looked at him. He did not persist. He got up, walked slowly out of the shop, and returned to the van. He headed downtown, for the Holland Tunnel in lower Manhattan, deciding that might be safer than the Lincoln Tunnel in midtown. It was barely a half hour since the murders, and over the van's radio came a constant stream of reports. He knew the alarm must be out, and he could not chance driving through the tunnel with Barbera's body in the back. He would have to get rid of it before he crossed into New Jersey.

Once in lower Manhattan, he drove around for a bit, stopping finally at a phone booth in front of a McDonald's, directly across the street from 26 Federal Plaza, the New York home of the Federal Bureau of Investigation. He called Dane again, and this time he followed an old habit of his when using a phone booth. He called the operator, gave her the number, and asked her to bill the call to his home phone in Keansburg. The New York Telephone Company made a record of the call. When he reached Dane, he said he was about to leave the city and wanted to make sure Dane would meet him as planned. Dane told him not to worry, he would be there.

There was still the question of what to do with Barbera's body. Driving up from Federal Plaza toward the Holland Tunnel entrance, he spotted a dim alley, Franklin Alley. He drove into it, opened the sliding side door of the van, and dumped the body well into the alley, then backed out and continued on his way, through the tunnel and out of New York.

Dane was waiting for him at the agreed spot. Nash ordered his nephew to follow him to Newark Airport. Once there, Nash drove into the long-term parking lot. Dane followed. Nash parked the van, got into Dane's car, and they drove out of the lot and headed for Keansburg.

Weeks later, Richie Chartrand questioned Thomas Dane about that meeting beside the parkway and that trip to and from Newark Airport. "Did you meet your uncle that night?" Chartrand asked.

"Yes, I met him," Dane said.

"And what was the topic of conversation?"

"Well, he told me that he's not happy at home and that he's going to leave his wife and going to go away."

"Then what did you do?"

"We went to the parking lot at the airport."

"You did?"

"Yeah."

"You brought Donald's other car with you?"

"Yeah."

"How did you get to the airport?"

"Well, Donald followed me."

"Well, what did he follow you in?"

"I don't know. I never paid any attention to what he was driving."

"So he just followed you in another vehicle?"

"Yeah."

"What other vehicles did he have access to?"

"Well, he had a taxicab and a van."

"Well, was he driving the van?"

"I don't know. I never saw."

"Well, now you go into the airport. You go in and he goes in and you come out and he doesn't. Did he leave the van there?"

"I guess so."

"Did you drive him from the airport?"

"I guess so."

"Why do you think he left the van there?"

"I don't know."

5

It was after midnight when Detectives Bobby Patterson and Eddie Fisher reached quiet, tree-lined Grandview Avenue in Ridgewood, Queens, a modest, middle-class neighborhood. They stopped in front of number 613, a low, nondescript apartment house indistinguishable from those around it, lining the streets of the area. All through the evening, Patterson had been dialing Barbera's telephone number. There was never an answer. From that and from what had been found on the pier, and from Sicca's story, it seemed likely that she was the woman who had been abducted and, perhaps, murdered. They had come in person now to find out if, indeed, the apartment was empty and she was missing. Cops from the 104th Precinct, which covered the area, were waiting for them. Patterson had called them to let them know he and Fisher were on the way and, because of jurisdiction, to ask them to meet the Midtown North detectives.

And then the case and the investigation became a little more complex and tangled, took on a new facet. The cops from the 104th knew Barbera, had come to know her very well over the past months. On January 5, her close friend, perhaps her only real friend, Jenny Soo Chin, a forty-six-year-old New Jersey housewife and sometime bookkeeper, had disappeared about seven in the evening after leaving Barbera's apartment, where she had spent the previous night. When Barbera learned that Chin had never reached her home in Teaneck and that her husband and four children had heard not a word from her, she got very worried. She went to the precinct and demanded an investigation, and in New Jersey, Chin's family reported her missing to the Bergen County authorities. But Barbera did not stop with a mere report. She posted fliers with Jenny Soo Chin's photograph and description on trees, lampposts, and in stores throughout Ridgewood, asking for information from anyone who might have seen anything that January evening. She hired a private detective to do a little investigating on his own. And she hounded the cops in the 104th, calling constantly, visiting often, incessantly prodding them to do something, anything, to find Chin.

At the 104th, Detective Rudy Gregorovic caught the missing-persons case. Over the next weeks, he went up and down Grandview Avenue and through the neighborhood, talking to everyone he could find. Nobody had seen anything. He, and the cops in Bergen County, talked to Edward Chin, Jenny Soo's husband, and to her sister and brother. The sister and brother were very concerned, wanted to help in any way they could, even offered to put up a reward for information. But Gregorovic and the New Jersey police, with whom he compared notes often, were struck by Edward Chin's stoical manner. He seemed bothered more by his wife's relationship with Barbera than by her disappearance. During the three years the two women had known each other, his wife had grown ever more dependent on Barbera, had spent more and more time with her, in her home in Teaneck and in Barbera's apartment in Queens, had taken a job Barbera had gotten for her, one she was not particularly qualified for, had gone on vacations and trips alone with her, had grown increasingly distant from her husband and family.

Nearly a week after Jenny Soo Chin vanished, what had appeared at first to be simply a missing-persons case, where the missing person might well have been missing because of her own actions and for her own personal reasons, took on a more troubling and serious complexion. On January 11, Chin's red Pontiac station wagon was found, abandoned, far west on Thirty-sixth Street in Manhattan, only a few blocks from the entrance to the Lincoln Tunnel. Inside, there were bloodstains on the door and window handles, on the armrest in the front, and on the carpet. And there was a spent .22-caliber shell casing on the floor in the front of the car. There was no sign of Jenny Soo Chin.

It was another two weeks before anyone learned anything more about her disappearance, and what they learned indicated violence, indicated that what had been found in that abandoned car in Manhattan might very well mean that Chin had vanished for good. These were weeks when Barbera did not let up on her steady badgering of the cops, who were making little prog-ress, and of her own private detective, who was making none at all. Two fourteen-year-olds, a boy and a girl, who lived on Grandview Avenue, were out that evening on their way to a friend's. They saw something that, initially, they paid little at-tention to. But then they saw the fliers that Barbera had plas-tered around the neighborhood. They called her. She called the 104th. Gregorovic went to talk to the teenagers. On that January evening, they told him, as they had been walking toward their friend's house, they had seen a woman who seemed to fit Chin's description walking along the avenue. A man was following her. She turned the corner into Linden Street and walked toward a station wagon parked a little way along the block. As she bent to unlock the car door, the man came up behind her, grabbed the door and pulled it open, threw her inside across the front seat, and jumped in after her. She screamed. The car door slammed, and a moment later, the car sped away. The man, they said, was tall and slim and had a dark ski mask pulled down over his head and face. Later, under hypnosis, the girl repeated the story and gave essentially the same description.

But when Gregorovic went back to the area and stood in the spot where they had been, at about the same time of night, he wondered about the description. They must have been at least a hundred feet from the station wagon, and the light was very dim. That they had seen something, and probably what they described, he did not doubt. But the description of the man? That kind of lighting can play tricks with the vision.

So Jenny Soo Chin was not only gone but also probably kidnapped and most assuredly seriously injured if not killed. The questions remained: Where was she, or her body? Who had done the violence? Some of the cops who had talked to him began to speculate about a possible role in all this for Edward Chin, given what seemed a very strained relationship with his wife. But it was only speculation, and nobody did much about it since there was nothing except that uneasy sense, and a statement by Barbera to Gregorovic that he ought to ask some hard questions of Edward Chin, to back them up.

By late February, Jenny Soo Chin had been gone for more than six weeks without a trace. Her family in New Jersey, and Barbera, hired a psychic, Dorothy Allison, to go on a hunt. Accompanied by cops from the 104th and from Bergen County, Allison directed a psychic hunt beginning at Barbera's apartment building in Queens, across the Fifty-ninth Street Bridge into Manhattan, and on to the spot on the West Side where the car was found. But all Allison could dig out of her psychic sense was a very strong feeling that Chin was in the water, but what water and where she didn't know.

More than a month later, that April night on the street in front of 613 Grandview Avenue, Patterson and Fisher heard all this from the cops of the 104th. And they heard something else. During one of her many conversations with Gregorovic and other cops, Barbera had said that she was somehow involved, perhaps as a witness, in a federal investigation. She didn't go into any detail and they didn't press the line, since it didn't seem to have anything to do with what they were investigating, Chin's abduction and disappearance.

Barbera's apartment was on the fourth floor of the building. Roused from sleep, the superintendent led them up the stairs and unlocked the door. The apartment was a one-room studio, with separate kitchen and bath. It was, Patterson remembers, "a mess. It was this tiny little apartment but it had like six rooms' worth of stuff crammed into it. The coffee pot was still going. The iron was plugged in. There was a cup of coffee on a little counter that had like two sips taken out of it. It appeared that somebody had left in a big hurry. We learned later that she had a habit of doing things like that, getting distracted and going out and leaving the iron and things on. She was that kind of person. We didn't know it then, of course, so we didn't know what to make of it. But looking around, it was obvious to me that to really do a thorough search of the place would have taken me at least a day, maybe two."

There wasn't time for that then, and they weren't there that night to do it. "We were really there only to look for clues, some identification. After all, we had a person who said he saw a woman being dragged into a van on the pier, and we had her car on the pier and her purse and things like that, and we traced the car back to her. So we figured it had to be her. We didn't know exactly what had happened to her, but we figured right from the start that she'd been abducted and maybe she was dead. So we were looking to get any information we could as far as her family and background were concerned, and we were looking for something to tie her in with somebody else, like boyfriends. As far as we knew then, it could have been a domestic kind of thing on the pier, a boyfriend who was angry with her or something like that."

They searched quickly, though "it was a kind of a half-assed search," Patterson says. When they opened a closet, they were staggered by the accumulation that piled, it seemed, almost from floor to ceiling, from front to back. There were mounds of stamps, for she was a stamp collector. There were piles of coins, for she was a coin collector. There was jewelry, and some of it looked very good and expensive. "We found bank statements all the way back to 1973 that she'd never opened. I guess she never bothered to open her bank statements. She just threw the envelopes into that closet when they arrived and forgot about them. We found income-tax returns she'd done for people and never bothered to send in. We found financial ledgers and records, but we didn't look through them. We found photographs, lots of them. There were the tourist kind, of things in Europe and other places. There were photos of her, though we didn't know that for sure at the time, but we figured it was probably her. We found a lot of photos of a Chinese woman, some of her alone and some of the two women together. We didn't know who the hell the Chinese woman was then. We took a bunch of the photos with us, along with some other stuff, so later we could match things up."

They found something else in that closet that surprised them and gave them pause. There were dozens of lesbian magazines and books, lavishly and explicitly illustrated and obviously well and often thumbed through.

Everything in that closet, like everything scattered around that small, cluttered apartment, was intensely private, not meant for prying eyes, left as it was because Barbera had not thought when she had closed the door behind her hours before on her way to work that anyone would invade her privacy, that someone would learn the secrets that were meant for no one else. But the dead, especially those who have met violent death, have lost the right of privacy, have no secrets. Their lives, the public and the hidden, are open to the lens of the police microscope, and every corner of their existence is searched minutely. The search, of course, is not one for some vicarious titillation; it is in the hope that behind those now-open doors may lurk the reasons for that sudden death, the clues that will lead to the unraveling of the mystery, the knowledge of what happened and why. So all that Margaret Barbera left behind, confident that it was hers and hers alone, now belonged to the public, the representatives of the public trying to solve her murder, if, indeed, she had been murdered. In the days and weeks to come,

in search after search through her possessions and her life,
images would form in the minds of those who had not known
her while she lived, and in those pictures might loom at least
some of the reasons for her violent end.

But that initial search turned up just a little, just enough
so that Barbera, if she was found, could be identified and somebody close to her notified. Then Patterson and Fisher locked
the apartment and left. They would return if they had to and
go through those belongings carefully and slowly. But not this
time. Before the night was out, they would be back again, and
in the days that followed, they would be in and out of that
apartment often.

At about five-thirty that morning, April 13, Manuel Infante, an aspiring abstract artist who supported himself as a
bartender, got to his apartment in lower Manhattan after a long
night of pouring drinks. He was ready for bed, but his German
shepherd demanded a walk first. Infante gave in to the dog's
demands, took him on that stroll through the dark of lower
Broadway. At the entrance to Franklin Alley, between Franklin
and White Street, the dog began tugging at the leash. Infante
gave it its head, followed the dog into the alley, where it began
sniffing at a heap off to one side. "I thought it was garbage,"
he said. "I went over to stop him. That's when I noticed the
body. At first I thought it was a bum sleeping. When I got close,
it didn't look like she was wearing dirty clothes. They looked
expensive. Then I touched the body with my finger and I realized she was dead."

A few minutes later, in Midtown North, Lieutenant Dick
Gallagher heard the news that the body of an unidentified woman
had been found in the alley. He had a hunch. He called down
to the local precinct. "The body you just found," he said, "is
she wearing shoes?" The woman, he was told, was shoeless.
"Don't do a thing," he said. "I'll be right there."

Gallagher sped through the dark streets before dawn, holding the shoes that had been found near Barbera's purse on the
pier. At the alley, he bent and tried the shoes on the body.
"They were," he says, "a perfect fit."

So Margaret Barbera had been found. She was dead. There was a bullet from a .22-caliber automatic in her head.

Just after nine that morning of April 13, New York City's chief of detectives, James Sullivan, called the head of the New York office of the Federal Bureau of Investigation. We had a murder last night, he said, four of them, in fact. The high FBI official had heard. We have a story, Sullivan said, that one of the victims may have been a witness in one of your investigations. Is there any truth to that story? The FBI official said he would check and get back to Sullivan.

Later that morning, FBI supervisor Don Richards and Special Agent Bob Paquette walked into the detectives' squad room of Manhattan North.

6

Late on the night of April 12, Donald Nash made a phone call. He rang the unlisted number of the Manhattan office of attorney Henry Oestericher. The office was closed by then, but an answering machine logged the call. It was urgent that Nash speak to Oestericher. He would contact him again in the morning.

Late that night, though, Oestericher did receive a call, at his home. The caller was Forty-seventh Street jewelry manufacturer Irwin Margolies, and he was calling from his home in Westchester County.

"Henry," Margolies said, "did you hear the news?"

"I heard," Oestericher said.

"Oy vey," Margolies said and hung up.

PART TWO

TWO

FRAUD

7

Irwin Margolies was a man desperately reaching for the gold ring on life's merry-go-round. There were some along West Forty-seventh Street in Manhattan, where he owned his own jewelry manufacturing business, and in the Westchester County suburb of Greenburgh (the unincorporated portion in which he lived had the post-office address of Scarsdale and hence seemed to share the outward semblance of wealth and exclusivity of this neighbor to the east), where he owned a sprawling home worth more than $200,000, who were sure he must have grasped it. After all, he had that business which, he told people, was not only very successful but also growing more so by the day. He owned that home. He dressed well and so did his wife, Madeleine, and their two sons, Steven and Douglas. He traveled the high road. He gave the impression of wealth and success.

Irwin Margolies liked to tell business friends that there were only two things that were worth anything—gold and diamonds, particularly diamonds. In a world of ever-shifting and changing values, they were what a man could depend on. Through the ages, all over the world, in the most primitive as well as the most advanced societies, people had yearned for them with a palpable ache, had stopped at nothing to get them. They had been the motives for crimes of every imaginable kind, they had been the reason for explorations, had been behind wars and the subjugation of nations. That wouldn't change. Tastes might change. Currencies might fluctuate wildly, worth a fortune one day and good only to paper walls the next. Civilizations might crumble and vanish. But the unquenchable thirst for diamonds and gold would always remain. Their value would only increase. And so, when a man possessed them, he had position, he had respect, he had power, he had safety, he had all he needed, and nothing could touch him.

This Irwin Margolies devoutly believed. The trouble was, his dream of riches, of hordes of diamonds and gold, remained only a dream, always just out of reach despite his outward pose. He had made a comfortable living as a jewelry salesman, but far from the fortune he craved. And so he thought perhaps if he started his own business, his luck would change. In 1974, he founded Candor Diamond Corporation, though at first it was only a shell, and it would be another four years before it began actual operations. And when it did, true, it dealt in items made of gold and encrusted with diamonds, but the gold was a mere wash across the surface of baser metals, and the diamonds that studded the rings, earrings, bracelets, broaches, necklaces, and the rest were far from top quality. And the output of Candor Diamond did not find its way into the windows and showcases of Tiffany and Cartier but rather into Army and Air Force PX's and such chain stores as Caldor and Ohrbach's and Alexander's, and sold not for thousands but for less than a hundred dollars.

By 1980, then in his midforties, a tall, obese man with thinning black hair, a thick black moustache, and small, cold eyes concealed behind thick spectacles, Margolies was just barely staying afloat, though he never abandoned the posture of affluence. The value of his Westchester home was strictly on paper. He had bought it long before, when prices were low, and had watched its worth spiral during the real-estate boom of the 1970s. In the new real-estate market of the early 1980s, he could never have afforded another even close to matching it and, besides, had he sold it, most of the money would have gone to pay off heavy first and second mortgages, in excess of $190,000, taken out partly to help finance the business. For, despite his claims, Candor Diamond was anything but a smashing success. It never had more than a half-dozen employees. Its sales fluctuated within a narrow range of $500,000 to $1 million a year, with minuscule profits. And Irwin and Madeleine Margolies, who worked together to try to make a go of the company, he as president, she as vice-president and secretary, never took home even $30,000 a year.

But Margolies was not a man to abandon dreams. He was forever searching for ways to take possession of the gold ring, and he didn't care whether the ways were ethical or patently illegal or somewhere just along the narrow line separating the two. As long as the scheme had a seeming viability that would trap the gullible, friend or stranger, Margolies was all for it.

For instance: In 1973, a year before the founding of Candor Diamond, Margolies embarked on another venture in manufacturing and wholesaling relatively inexpensive jewelry of original design. He and an old friend, Joseph Ingber, set up a company they called Monarch Designs. Ingber put up all the cash. Margolies put up his design ideas, his salesmanship, and $35,000 in promissory notes.

It all looked very good to Ingber. He trusted his partner, was confident in his abilities both as a designer and a salesman, and as an executive who would run the firm. And his confidence grew when he got a look at a sample line Margolies created. Ingber was sure it had enormous potential, and the $50,000 it had cost to produce that sample seemed as nothing if the jewelry touched a receptive chord with retailers and the public. That was supposed to be Margolies's next step, to take those samples around to jewelers, department stores, and other potential outlets and convince them they could make a fortune handling it.

But before any retailers had placed an order, before any had even gotten a glimpse of the Margolies creations, Ingber fell ill and was hospitalized with meningitis. While he was recovering, he heard that his partner, Margolies, and the sample case containing the $50,000 worth of jewelry had vanished. Enraged, Ingber called the Manhattan district attorney's office and his insurance company and told them his partner was a crook who had made away with the company's gems. The district attorney found Margolies. Margolies ingenuously and with certain outrage protested his innocence. Of course he had the sample case, he said. How else could he interest potential customers in the Monarch designs without it? If his partner, Ingber, had so little trust in him, then he would, of course, return the case to him and that would be that.

The case, however, did not appear at Monarch's offices, and neither did Margolies. As long as he was in the hospital, there was little else Ingber could do. But once he was cured, released from the hospital, and back at work, Ingber set out to find and confront his partner. Initially he had no success. Margolies was just not to be found anywhere. Then, one afternoon, he and one of his employees spotted the missing Margolies in a midtown Manhattan garage, waiting for an attendant to bring down his car. In one hand was the missing sample case. Ingber and his employee moved toward Margolies, faced him, and demanded the return of the case. Margolies took one look at them and raced from the garage and down the street. But a man of his bulk is neither agile nor fast, and before he had gone half a block, the two men in pursuit had caught up with him and had him pinned against a building wall. Margolies handed over the sample case and strode away as fast as he could.

But Ingber was not through with him. There still was the matter of Margolies's $35,000 promissory notes. Ingber was not going to let Margolies off the hook. He demanded payment. Margolies resisted. Monarch Designs was dead and, he claimed, he had little money, and, besides, the collapse of the business was really Ingber's fault for not trusting him. Ingber persisted. And then his phone began to ring, late at night, early in the morning, at odd hours. The caller was Margolies, and the words he spoke and the tone he used put inordinate fear into Ingber. Nothing, certainly not $35,000, was worth what Margolies was putting him through. And so when Margolies offered $1,200 as settlement for the notes, Ingber promptly accepted the offer.

For instance: A few months after the conclusion of the Monarch Designs affair, Margolies came up with another get-rich-quick scheme. He dropped in on an old acquaintance, Fred Modell, owner of Modell Jewelry, Inc. Margolies had, he said, just had a stroke of great fortune. He had taken over the jewelry concession at JGE Stores, then a very prosperous retail chain. As a result, he was calling on friends in the business with the idea that they might like to have him sell their products, on consignment. Modell, who, like so many others in those days, thought Margolies an upright and successful man of great promise, took to the idea and handed over $100,000 of Modell jewelry.

It was not long before Modell had reason to regret his trust. The agreement he had with Margolies provided that Margolies would regularly provide Modell with information on sales as well as payment for the items that were sold. But the reports just didn't arrive, and after a few months Modell told Margolies that the jewelry would have to be returned.

Margolies put up no argument. In fact, he told Modell, his concession with JGE was just not working out as well as he had hoped, and he was actually in the process of taking back the merchandise from the ten JGE outlets. Once he had the gems, they would be stored in his office on Fifth Avenue at Forty-seventh Street and then returned to Modell and others who had entrusted their products to him.

Modell waited. The jewelry never showed up. He called Margolies. Margolies apologized for the delay and set a date when he would return the gems to Modell. Came the day, and the jewels did not appear. What arrived was a sorrowful phone call from Margolies. A terrible thing had happened. During the previous night, someone had broken into his office and looted the safe. What could Margolies do? It was one of those

55

things. Perhaps the best thing would be for Modell to put in a claim with his insurance company. Modell not only did that, but he also called the cops. What he learned gave him pause. They were not conducting an active investigation of the reported burglary. Why? Modell asked. Because, he was told, their initial investigation had revealed no sign of damage to the Margolies office, no sign of forced entry into the safe—no sign, in fact, of a theft of any kind.

But Margolies insisted that there had been a burglary, that his safe had been broken into, and that Modell's goods had been stolen. With Margolies stonewalling that way, Modell had little choice but to take a small settlement from his insurance company, swallow the heavy loss on the $100,000 in merchandise, and vow never to do business with Irwin Margolies again.

For instance: Margolies did not forget his success with the Modell scam, and when the opportunity arose to play it again, he did not hesitate. It was six years later, on December 15, 1980. Candor was in operation then, a going concern, if not going very far or very fast. About four-thirty that morning, the burglar alarm in Candor's offices on West Forty-seventh Street went off in the headquarters of Jeweler's Protective Service, which was charged with protecting Candor's premises as well as those of scores of other operations in the diamond center. Jeweler's Protective might have the job of safeguarding the property, but Margolies had neglected to supply the agency with a key, so there was no way to get inside and find out if, indeed, something was wrong. The only alternative was to call the Margolies home in Westchester and tell them there might be some trouble at the office. Madeleine Margolies took the call. She sounded still half asleep. When she heard the news, she said there was nothing she or her husband could do about it at that hour. When they got to the office in the morning, they would check and get back to the agency.

In midmorning, Irwin Margolies called Jeweler's Protective. He was furious. He had been robbed, he raged. Somebody had broken into Candor Diamond through a rear window, which, somehow, had been left unlocked. That somebody had cracked the two safes in the manufacturing area and made away with diamonds, gold, and other valuables worth about $200,000.

To Jeweler's Protective, the whole thing emitted a foul stench. Nobody in the diamond business is so careless as to forget to lock the windows when the workday ends. Nobody in the diamond business ignores a summons about a possible burglary, no matter the hour. Nobody in the diamond business stores the valuables in the small safes in the work areas at the end of the day; they are used strictly in the daytime by workers making the jewelry. Come evening, everything is removed to larger and more secure safes in other parts of the office.

But Irwin Margolies shouted that he had been robbed and that his losses were staggering. He reported the burglary to the police, who investigated briefly but could find nothing to convince them that a crime had actually occurred. He reported the burglary to his insurance agent and said he wanted to file a claim for his $200,000 loss. The agent, Arthur Schwartz of Schwartz Hirtenstein and Company, who handles the insurance for many companies in the diamond center, was sympathetic. He told Margolies to put together an inventory of what had been stolen so that a proper claim could be filed, and then the insurance company would make good the loss. Somehow or other, Margolies just never got around to furnishing that inventory, despite a number of calls from Schwartz, and a short time later, he told the insurance agent that he had decided to take his loss in silence and was withdrawing his insurance claim. Schwartz was not a little surprised. He found it hard to remember another occasion when a client failed to follow through and pursue collection on his insurance when he had suffered a major burglary.

Margaret Barbera, the controller and keeper of the books of Candor Diamond and who by then had become a trusted employee of Margolies, would later offer an explanation. Margolies, she said, had come to her one day and told her of his plan to pretend that there had been a burglary and thus collect the $200,000 in insurance. What he wanted was her cooperation. She should prepare the inventory of fictitious items that he would say had been stolen and so satisfy the insurance company. She refused, Barbera claimed, and as a result, Margolies pulled back.

For instance: In May 1981, Margolies approached L. M. Van Mopes and Sons Ltd., a highly respected London-based diamond merchant. He was expanding, he said. He was about to turn out jewelry of a far better quality than he had in the past and, as a result, he needed very-good-quality diamonds. Of course, like most small businessmen in the business, his ready cash was tied up. Would Van Mopes take promissory notes in exchange for the diamonds, notes that would be paid off as soon as the new items were on the market, if not sooner? It was not an unusual request. Van Mopes agreed. It turned over $220,000 worth of high-quality diamonds to Margolies. He turned over $220,000 in promissory notes.

Over the next four months, the diamonds vanished and the promised payments never were made. Despite all its efforts, despite pressures and entreaties, Van Mopes learned that dealing with Irwin Margolies, that trying to make an impression on him, was like trying to make dents in the air. It was out the diamonds, and all it had to show for its trust was a handful of worthless paper.

To the world at large, Irwin Margolies held himself out as an honest and successful businessman, proprietor of a small but rapidly growing and profitable concern, devoted husband and father who provided his wife and children with all they could wish, devout Orthodox Jew who was dedicated to his religion and its commandments and moral precepts.

To some who dealt with him and who came to know what that meant over the years, however, Irwin Margolies was a devious and crooked man who would stop at little to reach his goals, who could never be trusted to keep his word, who traveled twisted paths in preference to straight ones, who broke without moral scruple any religious commandment that stood in his way. He was, someone would say later, one bad dude.

But still, he had his winning ways. He was a salesman who

could sell himself, who could convince people who should have known better that what he had to offer was the real thing, that the outward veneer was no veneer but solid all the way through.

And Irwin Margolies had a friend who, in 1980, showed him the way to make his dreams come true, finally to reach out and seize that prized gold ring.

8

Henry Oestericher was a few years older than Irwin Margolies. They had known each other for much of their lives, and their friendship had endured through the years. Like his old and close friend, Oestericher was a man with unrealized dreams. When he was young, he had dreamed of success and fortune in the jewelry business. He had grown up in it. His father was a prominent and successful jewelry merchant and manufacturer, had been one of the pioneers in the use of factoring—the borrowing of money secured by accounts receivable and anticipated sales—in the jewelry business to support the growth of his firm. But when the younger Oestericher tried his hand at the family trade, he failed.

He turned to the law, and fantasized of fame and fortune at the bar. But after a quarter of a century as an attorney, he still operated only from desk space granted him as a favor in the offices of other lawyers on West Forty-fourth Street just off Fifth Avenue. He had never handled a major case, either in court or in the office, was reduced to scratching for business wherever he could find it, was dependent to a large degree on the legal affairs thrown his way by Margolies, more out of that old and enduring friendship than because of any legal talents Oestericher might have revealed.

To support himself and his family, his legal practice providing only a meager income, far from enough for the life-style he aspired to and tried to maintain, Oestericher spent a good part of his working hours as a landlord's agent, managing buildings around New York and in New Jersey. But even here, his buildings were not in the luxury class, not along the Upper East Side or Upper West Side. They tended to the seedy, like the one on West Forty-fifth Street where Vinnie Russo maintained his catering establishment and where Donald Nash kept his desk and telephone. Oestericher managed a couple of apartments in New Jersey and, among others, the Somerset Hotel at Broadway and Forty-seventh Street, a fleabag cited too many times to count for violations of the buildings and sanitation codes, for nonpayment of taxes, and for scores of other infractions. And it was notorious as a haven for the neighborhood prostitutes; Oestericher's connection with it earned him, from some of the area's denizens, the nickname "The Pimp of Father Duffy Square," the statue of Father Duffy of World War I fame staring across at the Somerset.

Then, one day early in 1980, Henry Oestericher came up with an idea that might make all his dreams and those of his close friend come true.

As he sometimes did in private with somebody he could trust, with a close confidant, Margolies that day was bemoaning his fate to Oestericher. The business wasn't growing fast enough, was constantly teetering on the edge. He had been forced to mortgage his Westchester home to keep it afloat. He was constantly having to invent new and more outrageous scams to bilk the unwary and raise the needed cash, and a lot of them seemed to backfire, and certainly none brought in enough really to make the effort pay off as he wanted. What he needed was a foolproof scheme that would bring in enough so that he would never have to worry again.

Oestericher listened. He had heard the story before, was

well aware of what lengths Margolies had been driven to, was willing to go to, and was capable of. He knew, too, or he expected that if he could come up with the scheme that would help Margolies, he would gain his own reward. It had been on his mind for some time. Now was the time to spell it out.

What did Margolies know about factoring?

Margolies knew enough to know that it was a major financing method in the garment industry; it was the way those companies, trapped in a seasonal business, were able to get the cash to turn out new lines every season.

Had Margolies thought about going to a factor to finance his jewelry manufacturing business?

Margolies had not. Factoring was not a particularly common practice in the jewelry business, though it was done. Besides, Candor Diamond was a small company without much of a growth record. It was doubtful if one of the major factors would jump at the chance to finance his accounts.

Don't be too sure, Oestericher said. He himself knew plenty about factoring. After all, his father had been one of the earliest jewelry merchants to go that way. Perhaps Margolies was right that one of the long-established jewelry factors might look the other way if he approached. But, Oestericher said, he knew of a factor who might just leap at the chance. John P. Maguire and Company, the factoring division of Irving Trust Company, had, for some years and with considerable success, financed garment firms. But it was anxious to spread itself out from that highly volatile industry into one that might be less seasonal and a little more secure. Garments were garments, and if a line flopped, the factor was left holding a lot of cloth and some clothes that nobody wanted, and it would be lucky if it could sell off for pennies on the dollar. But the jewelry business was something else again. If the earrings and bracelets and broaches and other trinkets didn't sell, there were always the diamonds and the gold and the other jewels used to make them. They didn't lose their value. They always could be sold, and they would bring plenty on the market and so would be a protection against major losses. Oestericher knew people at John P. Ma-

62

guire, knew how anxious they were to get a foot in the door of a new market for their money. Would Margolies like an introduction? Or, better still, why didn't he have his Scarsdale bank, which held the second mortgage on his home, make the opening contacts and thus provide an element of stability and probity?

The more Margolies listened, the more he liked the whole idea. He and Oestericher were not, that day, merely talking about finding a new source of funds to support Candor Diamond and help it grow, of course. What they were talking about, and both men knew it, was a scheme to take John P. Maguire not for thousands but for millions.

Soon after that discussion, Margolies approached officers of Scarsdale National Bank, told them he had heard that John P. Maguire might be interested in factoring jewelry manufacturers. Since he personally didn't know anybody there, would the bank make the necessary introductions? Scarsdale National was more than happy to comply. Within a few weeks, Margolies was deep in discussions with Maguire.

On March 21, 1980, the negotiations were completed to everyone's satisfaction, and a contract was signed between Maguire and Margolies. Under the agreement, Maguire would advance Candor Diamond up to 85 percent of the sales price of its merchandise, the money to be transferred to Candor's account electronically once Candor Diamond shipped its merchandise to its customers and received invoices that would then be forwarded to Maguire. In exchange, Margolies personally guaranteed his company's debts to Maguire, and Candor Diamond gave Maguire a lien on its entire inventory of diamonds, gold, and other valuable gems and merchandise. Further, all the income from Candor Diamond's sales was assigned to Maguire. Candor Diamond's customers were to be notified, by a sticker pasted on the invoices and bills, that the company's sales were factored and that all payments were now to be made not to Candor Diamond but directly to Maguire, were to be mailed when due, normally within thirty to ninety days, to a post office lock box maintained by Maguire.

There was nothing unusual about the agreement; it was

the standard way that factoring worked. Maguire had no suspicion that anything out of the ordinary was about to take place, for Margolies and his company came highly recommended. (Margolies's past shady dealings and practices escaped Maguire's notice, if the factor even bothered to check.) In fact, if anything, Maguire was delighted with the whole arrangement. It was, company officials hoped, the opening into a new market for their money.

For Margolies, though, the arrangement was the golden ring he had long been reaching for. He was about to become a millionaire, at Maguire's expense. Initially he moved slowly and cautiously, and with a certain circumspection, like a swimmer testing with his toe the temperature of the water. He made his sales, shipped his goods, filed his invoices, and then received, into Candor Diamond's new bank account at Irving Trust (within six months, though, he would close that account and open a new one for Candor, somewhat farther from Irving Trust's reach, at Bank Leumi Trust Company in New York), from Maguire an amount equal to 85% of the sales prices noted on the invoice.

And then, on May 8, he tried a little experiment in fraud. He sent Maguire an invoice declaring that he had just sold and shipped to The Diamond Shop in St. Louis a batch of jewelry worth $7,704. Within a few days, Candor Diamond's account was $6,548.40 richer. The only thing was, The Diamond Shop had never ordered nor received any merchandise from Candor Diamond.

Margolies waited to see whether anybody at Maguire would catch wise, would ask any embarrassing questions. Nobody did. Of course, there still was the question of the payment of $7,704 to Maguire within about ninety days. Margolies figured that he would come up with a solution to that when the time came. What he knew now was that all he had to do was file invoices and Maguire would come up with 85% of the money. If he worked it right, Candor Diamond could become a giant within a very short time, a giant on paper and in the bank, of course, even though nobody in the marketplace ever saw much of its output.

But Margolies was not fool enough to think he could go on this way forever. Someday, of course, Maguire would catch wise and come down on Candor Diamond, demanding an accounting. When it did, somebody was going to go to prison. What Margolies needed was a patsy to take the fall when that day arrived.

9

Margaret Barbera was very good with numbers. She could take a balance sheet, a set of account books, invoices, bills, and more, juggle and manipulate the figures, and, presto, thousands became millions, losses became profits, profits became losses, sales soared or fell, whatever her employer desired, and it would take an expert auditor knowing precisely where to look and what to look for to figure out what she'd done, and even then, it still might slip by. There is an underground of people like Margaret Barbera, eagerly sought after by businessmen in trouble, especially in volatile and unstable industries such as garments and jewelry. Ask the right questions of the right people, and pretty soon a Margaret Barbera, or somebody very much like her, will come knocking at the door.

She had grown up in New York City, in the outlying boroughs of Brooklyn and Queens, child of a large nomadic family—some would say they were much like Gypsies, residing for a time in her childhood in the back of a small truck parked in vacant lots and at curbs, constantly on the move around the city, picking up work and dollars wherever they could be had.

Margaret was the smart one in the family. She was good at figures and was adept at figuring out the angles. When she graduated from high school in 1961, she got a job as a bookkeeper for a major chain store, worked there for a couple of years, and then moved on to mastering computers. But without a college education, she complained, her chances for advancement, for a good job at high pay, were strictly limited. So at twenty-seven, still holding down a full-time job, she got herself an apartment in Ridgewood, Queens, where she would remain until her murder, and went back to school, enrolling in the School of Commerce at New York University. She graduated in three years, with honors and a bachelor's degree in business administration. For another year, she was in graduate school at New York University, but then dropped out. Her grades had fallen sharply and, she told someone, besides, she felt she had learned about all the school had to teach her.

It was 1974 then, and she was a very busy lady. During the day she worked as an accountant for a large midtown company, and at night, in her Ridgewood apartment, she began to develop the skills that would bring her to the attention of needy businessmen. At her daytime job, she was earning $17,000. Nobody knows how much she was taking in at her after-hours work, but what is obvious is that it was occupying more and more of her time and energy, enough so that she was constantly inventing excuses for absences from her regular job. She compiled a long, sad story of constant and unrelenting bad luck. Her mother had cancer, she explained, and so she had to go and take care of her. Other relatives suddenly had fallen seriously ill, and she had been called on to tend them. She herself was ill—with cancer, with a variety of other ailments, serious and not so serious, and she was under treatment, which meant she could not go to work. Her fiancé (a man nobody who knew her seemed aware of) had been killed in an automobile accident and she was in mourning, too stricken to reach the office. By 1977 it had all become too much for her employer, and he felt he had no choice but to let her go.

For the next three years she worked sporadically as an

accountant at jobs she picked up through a temporary agency. At night and at other times she continued to ply her growing expertise in less legitimate accounting methods. She, too, it seemed, was waiting for the right moment, the right thing.

Her personal life was an enigma. Obviously she was earning a lot of money at her spare-time vocation, but what she was doing with it, nobody seemed to know. And nobody seemed to know her. Although she had lived for a decade in the same fourth-floor walk-up apartment, her neighbors knew her not at all. Sometimes they saw her on the stairs, passed by, nodded, but she never spoke a word. All any of them knew was that she had few visitors, only one with any regularity, an Oriental woman who arrived and often spent several days. And that was all.

In the spring of 1980, when Irwin Margolies began looking for an expert with figures to help him take John P. Maguire, someone who would become the patsy to take the fall when that day came, Margaret Barbera was exactly what he was looking for. As he had been throughout all his initial dealings with Maguire, Margolies moved with a certain caution. He asked his own auditors, H. W. Freedman Company, if they might happen to know a good accountant who wanted a job. Candor Diamond, he explained, was on the verge of major expansion, its business beginning to show substantial growth that should continue far into the future. As a result, the ledgers and books, the invoices and billings, all the record-keeping was going to be a very complicated matter. He needed somebody who could keep track of it all; there were going to be the government tax people and the state tax people and Maguire and a lot of others who were going to have to be kept informed, and informed correctly. He just wasn't going to have the time to take care of all this himself; he was going to be too busy designing and supervising the manufacturing and the selling. So he had to have somebody who was good and who was reliable. It just so happened that at that very moment, Margaret Barbera was working at Freedman on one of her temporary jobs. She seemed to know her business; she seemed reliable; she seemed just the kind of person to send along, with high recommendations, to Freedman's client, honest Irwin Margolies.

But Margolies was not about to take Barbera on Freedman's word alone. If she was all Freedman said, she certainly was not what Margolies had in mind. He did a little quiet checking among some like-minded friends. Did they know Margaret Barbera? What kind of person was she? Could she be depended on? Would she follow orders? The questions, subtly put, of course, were the tip-off as to what he meant, and the responses he elicited more than satisfied him. Detective Richie Chartrand later learned the identity of at least one of those who had given Margolies the good word about Barbera. "I knew the guy who referred her," he says. "I'm sure his recommendation was of the highest. I'm sure that knowing Irwin and what Irwin must be looking for, he said she was just the right kind of person. I wouldn't believe a word he ever said. One time he got robbed. They took everything he ever owned. He said, 'They held me up at gunpoint one night and I only had two Manhattans. They took all my goods. My watch.' But they didn't take his wedding ring. My God. You being robbed, they want to take your stuff, they'll take your wedding ring, they'll cut your finger off to get it. So if you're looking for a special kind of thing and he knows it, he's the right person to go to."

And so, at the beginning of June 1980, Margaret Barbera went to work for Margolies and Candor Diamond as a part-time bookkeeper. All the pieces of Margolies's plan were now in place. He had Maguire, which appeared by its actions, or inactions, over the first months of the factoring agreement, not merely gullible but almost anxious to be swindled, so pleased to have taken the first step into a new factoring market that it would be a long time, if ever, before anyone there had any suspicions or asked any questions. He had someone to doctor his books and to appear, on the surface at least, a responsible party. But when the crunch came, she would be his pigeon. It was, then, time to grow, time to become rich.

10

No sooner was Margaret Barbera at work than Irwin Margolies sat her down and explained exactly what he wanted. She had no qualms. She had done it for others and been well rewarded, and now she would do it for him, doctor his books and records expertly and gain additional rewards.

But Margolies had a problem, as he explained to Barbera. Some of the phony invoices he had sent on to Maguire were about to come due for payment. Did she have any ideas how to handle that? She did, indeed. Why not, she suggested, just send Maguire a Candor check for the amount?

It was a potential solution, one worth trying. Of course, according to the factoring agreement, the checks to Maguire were supposed to come from Candor's customers, not Candor itself. Would Maguire notice the discrepancy? Margolies wrote out the check, Madeleine Margolies signed it, and then it was sent to the Maguire post office lock box. Margolies waited anxiously to see whether anybody at Maguire would notice, whether anybody would call and say, "Mr. Margolies, there's been a mistake; this isn't the way it's supposed to be done under our contract; we're not supposed to get the checks from you; your customers are supposed to pay us directly; please make sure it doesn't happen again." But nobody complained. Perhaps nobody at Maguire noticed. Or perhaps somebody did notice but decided to ignore what might, after all, just be a minor peccadillo. After all, Maguire was delighted to have gained entrée into a new factoring market, and it was anxious not to do anything that might get in the way of expansion there. Whatever, it was precisely what Margolies had hoped and hardly dared expect, and what Barbera had predicted.

The door was wide open now, and Margolies strode boldly and confidently through it. Since its inception, Candor Diamond's sales pattern had been essentially flat, hovering at about $500,000 annually. Suddenly it was as though a rocket had been attached to its tail and ignited. The company became, according to the invoices it filed with Maguire, a lot more successful than anybody could have dreamed possible, its sales soaring into the stratosphere at a pace anybody who gave it some thought might have considered neither possible nor logical. But apparently nobody thought very hard about it, if they thought about it at all.

Aided and abetted by Barbera and her fertile imagination, Margolies took off in several directions. Behind it was an adaptation of the scheme hatched and brought to a certain perfection in the 1920s by Charles Ponzi in Boston: Pay the investor back with his own money, only make sure he keeps on investing at an ever-increasing rate so that the debt never catches up with the income. If it's done right and with panache, it will be a long time before the investor catches wise that all he's getting back is his own money from earlier, smaller investments.

On more occasions than not, Margolies simply ignored the stricture to paste the Maguire sticker to his invoices and bills, telling the customers that the sales were factored and that payments should be made not to Candor but directly to the Maguire post office lock box. So the bills—the legitimate ones, at least

—continued to go out as always and the customers continued to pay Candor, and then Candor paid Maguire. Only once did anyone at Maguire notice that Margolies was violating the rules and raise a howl. In November 1980, Peter O'Neill, the Maguire officer handling the Candor account, came across one of those Candor checks sent in to pay for an invoice that had been assigned to the factor. O'Neill immediately called Margolies and demanded an explanation. Margolies, with his salesman's winning ways, calmed O'Neill. What had happened, he explained, was that the customer hadn't followed directions and had sent his check to Candor. Rather than go to the bother of sending the check back and making the customer write and dispatch a new one, Margolies simply had deposited the check in the Candor account and written his own to Maguire. O'Neill was appeased. But he warned Margolies not to let it happen again. If it did, Maguire might consider that grounds for ending the factoring agreement. Margolies was not at all concerned. Too many checks had already slipped past Maguire for him to think that O'Neill's catching this one had been anything but an accident that was unlikely to happen often, if ever again. Margolies just ignored O'Neill's warning and continued to do as he had been doing, only more so.

If he could get away with continuing to collect as always from his legitimate customers and writing his own checks to the factor, then he had a clear road into the Maguire treasury to stage a raid on a massive scale. Like a magician pulling rabbits out of a hat, Margolies seemingly pulled names out of directories. Some were the names of retail stores with which Candor had never done any business, or had done no business in a long time, or had done business only on a minimal scale. Onto invoices went their names, showing that they were now making ever-increasing purchases from Candor. Off to Maguire went the invoices. Into Candor's bank account went 85% of the sales figure listed on the invoice.

That was one way. There were others. Candor sent off invoices to Maguire showing that it had made large sales of jewelry to such firms as Paramount Gems, Palazzo D'Oro, and

72

others. The only problem was that they weren't retailers. They were suppliers to Candor of diamonds, gold, and other materials and so, of course, were not in the market for Candor's goods.

Candor sent off invoices to Maguire showing that it had sold and shipped a large quantity of jewelry to a company called M & M Merchandising. What it didn't tell Maguire was that M & M Merchandising just happened to be a shell company owned by Madeleine Margolies's parents, Herman and Molly Malen, and that among the officers of M & M were Irwin and Madeleine Margolies.

In October 1980 it appeared that Candor had scored a real coup. It dispatched to Maguire invoices amounting to $250,000 for the purported sale and shipment of jewelry to Venture Stores. As ever compliant, Maguire deposited $212,500 into Candor's account, representing 85 percent of the sale. What Margolies neglected to tell Maguire was that the shipment was on consignment, not a true sale, and, for obvious reasons, since no money changes hands and no bills are rendered on consignments until the sale is made, consignments were specifically excluded from the factoring agreement.

Three months later, as the payment from Venture Stores to the Maguire lock box was supposedly due, somebody at Maguire made a call and inquired when that payment might be expected. The people at Venture Stores were not a little surprised. For one thing, they had never been told by Margolies that his sales were factored and payments were to be made to Maguire. For another, as they now informed Maguire, there had been no true sale anyway, only a consignment. To prove their point, they displayed the invoice sent them by Margolies, showing the shipment had been on consignment. That, of course, was not the same invoice that had been sent to Maguire.

The factor immediately called Margolies and demanded an explanation. Margolies said he was shocked. He said he had supplied Maguire with the correct invoice showing the shipment had been a sale. Venture Stores must be mistaken.

We've seen a copy of the invoice in their possession, Maguire said. It shows a consignment, not a sale.

That doesn't jibe with my invoices, Margolies declared. And he produced photocopies of the invoices in his possession. They showed that the merchandise had been shipped and sold to Venture Stores.

It was his word against that of Venture Stores, then. Margolies decided not to take a chance on which one Maguire would believe. He told his friend and attorney Henry Oestericher that his credibility and the continued success of the scheme were at stake. He ordered Oestericher to file a civil suit against Venture Stores, asserting that the chain had violated its purchase agreement with Candor, and he promptly notified Maguire that he was taking this action. If Maguire had been about to bring the factoring agreement to a sudden and decisive end as a result of the Venture Stores disclosure, this stopped them. If Margolies was taking this kind of action, then, Maguire officials reasoned, they must be dealing not with a crook but with honest Irwin Margolies, a man wronged by his customer. And so the agreement, and Margolies's raid on the Maguire treasury, continued unabated.

And a raid it was. By the end of 1980, according to the invoices sent to Maguire, which Maguire honored by depositing the required funds to Candor's account, the jewelry company's sales had more than doubled over the year before, reaching $1.2 million from about $500,000. Nobody at Maguire expressed surprise or suspicion. This was just the beginning. As the year turned into 1981, Candor's sales, as reported to Maguire, began to grow almost geometrically month after month. In May 1980, for instance, as the factoring agreement was in its germinal stages, Candor reported sales to Maguire of $41,000; a year later, in May 1981, it claimed sales of $1.393 million. In July 1980, as Candor was in the initial stages of its sudden and phenomenal growth spurt, it told Maguire its sales had reached $87,000 that month. A year later, in July 1981, it claimed sales of more than $2.4 million. All told, between May 1980 and July 1981, a period of just fourteen months, Margolies sent Candor invoices to Maguire claiming sales of about $10 million, nearly $9 million in the first half of 1981 alone. In return, Candor and Margolies received about $8.5 million from Maguire, most of it in the spring and early summer of 1981.

How explain such a fantastic sales growth? Margolies explained it easily, telling Maguire's Peter O'Neill one day that his company was booming at such a rate because the beautiful designs and high quality of the merchandise were creating great demand, and even more, because Margolies's own brilliant salesmanship had won some very large accounts.

Did anyone doubt? Margolies was prepared to show that the shipments were pouring out of the office. In early November 1980, for instance, Peter O'Neill announced that he would like to come into the Candor office and spend a day matching purchase orders and delivery documents against the invoices Candor had submitted regarding certain very large sales to the Caldor chain. Margolies had to oblige him. According to Gaye Broffman, who was working as Madeleine Margolies's assistant office manager at the time (a position she held for only a few months, between August and November 1980, when she departed with a certain distaste for what she had been witnessing), she had gone into the office on a Sunday to catch up on some paperwork. As she was getting ready to leave late in the afternoon, Irwin and Madeleine Margolies and Margaret Barbera stopped her. They asked her if she could stay on for a few more hours to do some essential work relating to O'Neill's expected arrival the following morning. What essential work? It seemed, Margolies said, that the original documents relating to delivery of merchandise to Caldor had been misplaced during Candor's recent move from one side of Forty-seventh Street to the other. What would have to be done was to prepare copies of Federal Express and Purolator delivery forms showing that the merchandise had been shipped from Candor to Caldor. Through the evening and into the morning, and when it became obvious that she couldn't finish the job alone, with the help of a friend Barbera asked her to recruit, Broffman typed hundreds of such delivery forms and then, on Barbera's orders, forged signatures of courier employees to every form. By the time O'Neill arrived, everything was in order.

Five months later, in April 1981, when Maguire officials

announced that they wanted to make another inspection, the forgery party was repeated, this time by Irwin and Madeleine Margolies and their two teenage sons, along with Madeleine Margolies's brother, Scott Malen, who was working as a Candor salesman, and Barbera.

When it came to repaying Maguire for its advances as they came due, Margolies showed equal ingenuity. The main method, of course, was the simple formula of writing Candor checks in payment for supposed sales. Margolies was certain that, despite the one occasion when O'Neill had voiced his displeasure at this violation of the contract, nobody at Maguire would notice that the checks were coming from Candor and not its customers, that in the main Maguire would be concerned only with getting what it was due when it was due and not about the source, and in keeping on the good side of a company that was becoming such a valuable client.

Even so, there were occasions when Margolies did call Maguire to explain why some checks had been drawn on Candor's account and not sent directly by the customers. The customers, he explained, had mistakenly sent their checks to Candor, and Candor's new and inexperienced bookkeeper (Barbera) had mistakenly deposited them in Candor's account at Bank Leumi. To save time, Margolies said he had simply issued offsetting checks to Maguire.

On at least one occasion, he even offered documentary evidence to prove that this was exactly what had happened. Late in October 1980, as payments for a number of invoices were coming due, Margolies withdrew $60,000 in cash from Candor's account at Bank Leumi. Immediately the cash was deposited into Madeleine Margolies's personal checking account at Scarsdale National Bank. Just as promptly, Madeleine Margolies wrote thirty-four checks, totaling $60,000, on that account and deposited them in Candor's Bank Leumi account, each check matching the purchase price on an invoice. Then she wrote thirty-four Candor checks to Maguire and noted on the checks the invoice number. And so Candor had the documentary evidence, in the form of the deposit slips, to show that the customers' checks had been put into Candor's account by mistake.

In all, during the fourteen months, Candor dispatched 177 of its checks, totaling about $3 million, to Maguire's lock box in payment of advances.

But this was only one ploy. Margolies and his reliable aide, Barbera, developed others as well, to convince the people at Maguire that at least some of Candor's customers were paying attention to the stickers on the invoices and remitting payments directly to the factor. One way was a check swap with officials of other firms with whom he was on friendly terms either socially or professionally. For reasons he hardly ever bothered to explain, he would approach a friend and say, "Let's swap checks, I'll give you my check for twenty thousand dollars, and you give me your check for twenty thousand dollars." It was a fair exchange, and who knew what business reasons a man like Margolies might have for suggesting something like that? Few turned him down. He did it with Paramount Gems and Palazzo D'Oro and with the family-owned shell, M & M Merchandising. He even did it with a man named Harry Ingber, owner of Carat Diamond Corporation and the brother of Joseph Ingber, the man Margolies had bilked in the aborted joint venture, Monarch Designs. One day in the fall of 1980, Margolies approached Harry Ingber and suggested that they swap checks for $22,000. Ingber agreed. Margolies endorsed the check and then sent it along to the Maguire lock box. What Ingber didn't know was that Margolies had sent Maguire an invoice three months earlier declaring that he had sold and shipped $22,000 worth of jewelry to Carat Diamond. That, in fact, was true in the case of all the check-swapping episodes. And so Maguire got checks for its full amount on the accounts of firms that Margolies supposedly had sold jewelry to. With that, Maguire became convinced the sales were genuine and, in these cases at least, Candor was following instructions.

With Candor's phenomenal growth, there always was the danger that the tax men might one day appear at the door and want a close look at the books to see what such a growing and profitable company owed the United States and New York State. Margaret Barbera took care of that. She kept multiple sets of books. One was an honest one and it showed that, despite the impression that was being given to Maguire, Candor was what Candor always had been. But then there were the books that would be shown to Maguire's auditors and tax people, should they ask. Here Barbera carefully listed every sale assigned to Maguire, in one the bogus sales, in another the real ones, in a third lumped together. Other books detailed the costs to Candor for the purchase of materials to make its jewelry; again the costs for the real jewelry, the costs for the bogus jewelry, and then combined costs. And lo and behold, in the books that were available to Maguire, to Candor's auditors, and to the government, the cost of raw materials matched the income from sales, and hence there were no profits.

But profits there were, for when it came to the fictitious sales there were no raw-material costs, for there was no merchandise. What arrived from Maguire, as advances against these fictions, was pure profit. And after paying something—about $3 million—back to Maguire as accounts became due, Irwin and Madeleine Margolies had, by early July 1981, nearly $5.5 million to do with as they would.

Jenny Soo Chin

Margaret Barbera

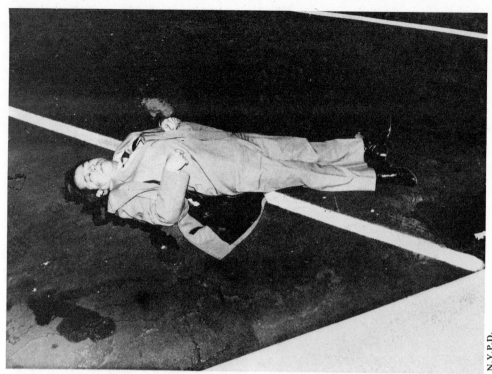

Body of Leo Kuranski

Body of Robert Schulz

Body of Edward Benford

Glasses, shoes, headband, and an unidentified towel are the only clues to the
abduction of Margaret Barbera.

Looking east from the rooftop garage toward the lights of Manhattan's sky-
scrapers. The body of Edward Benford can be seen to the left.

N.Y.P.D.

The cars of the murdered CBS employees are still parked side by side the morning after the killings.

The body of Margaret Barbera was discovered at 6 A.M. that morning.

The kitchen of Margaret Barbera proved to be as messy as her life. Note the *Federal Tax Handbook* lower right.

N.Y.P.D.

FORENSIC REPORT

PD321-091(4/72)

COMPLAINT NO.	PCT.	DETECTIVE DISTRICT		DATE OF REPORT	CRIME LAB NO. (IF ANY)	RUN NUMBER
5081	1	1 P.D.U.		4/16/82		82/998

OFFENSE			TIME NOTIFIED	TIME RESPONDED	TIME COMPLETED
HOMICIDE			0640	0655	1015

DATE & TIME OF OCCURRENCE	PLACE OF OCCURRENCE		APT/FLOOR
4/13/82 0600	Rear of 369 Broadway Alley		

NAME OF ☐ COMPLAINANT ☒ DECEASED	SEX	COLOR	DATE OF BIRTH	ADDRESS	PHONE NO.
MARGARET BARBERA	F	W	38 yrs.		

DEFENDANT'S NAME	ADDRESS	DATE OF BIRTH	ARREST NO.	"B" NUMBER

SUMMARY OF CASE

On April 13, 1982 at 0640 hrs. received a telephone message from Det. Walsh requesting the investigatory services of the Crime Scene Unit at the scene of a homicide located in the rear of 269 Broadway.

On April 13, 1982 at 0655 hrs. arrived at the requested location and received the following information from Det. Worth. At 0600 hrs. the unidentified body of a female-White was discovered in the rear of 369 Broadway. The deceased was face down and had rags covering the upper portion of her body.

FINGERPRINTS OR PHOTOGRAPHS

NO.	AREA/ITEM PROCESSED	AGENT/PROCEDURE USED	RESULTS NEG./POS.

A later examination of the deceased by this detective disclosed a hair present inside her right hand. She had a bullet wound entry in the back of her head at the base of her skull. A blue piece of plastic was present on the front of her skirt. Similiar pieces were present near her feet. Two pieces of foil/like material were present on the front of her clothing. Tire impressions were visible in the recently poured concrete and on two pieces of paper. Cloth similiar to that used to cover the deceased, was present in the rear of 373 Broadway.

Based on the information received and the observations made the following investigative services were performed.

PHOTOGRAPHS:

1. Franklin Ave. from Franklin St. towards White St.
2. Franklin Alley from White St. towards Franklin St.
3. Rear of 373 Broadway towards 269 Broadway
4. Franklin Alley showing the rear of 369 Broadway and the deceased
5. Body
6. Close-up of drag markes on the heels of the deceased
7. Close-up of inpression of skirt
8. Close-up showing plastic, hands and face
9. Tire impressions from the rear of 373 Broadway
10. Tire impression on paper bag
11. Tire impression of paper

FINGERPRINTS:

The box from which the cloth used to cover the deceased was processed for the presence of latent fingerprints with negative results.

NO. SCENE NEGATIVES:	BLACK/WHITE		COLOR		FINGERPRINT PHOTOS/NEGATIVES	ELIMINATIONS/SUSPECTS ☐ YES ☐ NO SEE OVER
VEHICLE EXAMINATION					NAME/ADDRESS OF OWNER	

YEAR	MAKE	LICENSE NO.	ODOMETER		

SAFE EXAMINATION - TYPE	HOW OPENED	TRACE MATERIAL COLLECTED

OTHER EVIDENCE	LOCATION	DISPOSITION

RANK/NAME ASSIGNED DETECTIVE	SHIELD	COMMAND	RANK/NAME TECHNICIAN & ASSISTANT	SHIELD
Det. Chartrand			Det. James F. Sullivan 2318 Det. Donald Green	

N.Y.P.D.

11

Irwin and Madeleine Margolies had suddenly become very rich, beginning in the late summer and early fall of 1980. And they began to live as they had always dreamed of living, as the millionaires they now were. Like many of the *nouveau riche*, they could not resist the temptation to flaunt their newfound wealth, and they threw cash in every direction.

They gave themselves substantial raises from the business, of course. In the past, their combined incomes from Candor had never reached even $30,000 a year. Now each was earning about $40,000 a year. But that was only the beginning. They tapped the Candor bank account for another $85,000 in cash, for personal expenses, and they had Candor pick up all their credit-card charges. In fact, they used the Candor accounts as if they were their own personal ones, Candor checks and Candor cash flowing out to pay for everything they wanted.

And there was almost no limit to what they wanted. They wanted cars. Candor bought them cars, three Porsches for more than $150,000, and that was only the start. Madeleine Margolies wanted a smaller car, so Candor bought her a Mercury Capri for $12,000. That was in addition to an Audi 5000 and a Pontiac Firebird Trans Am. Even that wasn't enough. They needed limousines and cars for special occasions, so they rented them when the time was right and filed the charges, $3,500 all told, with Candor.

They joined the Imperial Yacht Club, so, of course, they had to have a boat. They spent $24,000 of Candor's cash for a thirty-two-foot cabin cruiser and moored it at the yacht club's marina. But here, they tried a little subterfuge. On the yacht club's records, they changed the boat's registration after a couple of months, claiming the owner was a man named James Lerner, who, the records showed, happened to live at their address. James Lerner was a social acquaintance. But about the boat and the fact that it was registered in his name, he knew nothing, and when he learned about it, he was more than a little distressed.

They decided to redecorate their Greenburgh home, so they hired an interior decorator, paying her, in cash, about $7,500 for the job. Candor's cash, too, went for thousands more in new furniture, and there was an $18,000 bill for new plush carpeting. Much later, Detective Richie Chartrand had an opportunity to view the inside of the Hadden Road house along with some FBI agents. "The inside was beautiful," he remembers. "I was very impressed, particularly with the bedroom. They had a platform bed and raised into the air they had television sets on tracks, two of them, with remote controls up to the bed so that Irwin could lie in bed and his bride could lie in bed and they had their own televisions and they could look at different programs and could control the angles of the television sets as well as the channel selections. I thought it was beautiful and I wanted to make him an offer on the house, but I was told that wouldn't be proper."

Candor, of course, did more than merely redecorate and refurnish the Margolies home. It also paid about $48,000 on the mortgage and another $4,250 for a maid to keep the house clean.

Then there was a condominium in Fort Lauderdale, Fla. Irwin and Madeleine Margolies had gone to Florida in early February 1981 to visit Madeleine's parents, Herman and Molly Malen, and to take a little vacation from all the hard work and pressure of running their successful operation. They decided while there that maybe it would be a good idea if they made a little investment, bought a condominium. They looked around and soon found one they thought ideal. The price was $152,500, and they offered no arguments. Madeleine wrote a couple of checks, for the 10 percent down payment of $15,250, on her personal account at Scarsdale National Bank, and the couple agreed to come up with the balance of $137,250 at the closing on June 15. The only problem with the down payment was that Madeleine didn't happen to have enough in her personal account at that moment to cover the checks she had written. That, naturally, was no problem. Candor simply deposited $17,000 in her Scarsdale account to cover the checks.

The balance for the closing was something else, though. The Margolieses already were pulling so much out of the Candor account that to take another $137,250 out at one time might arouse somebody's suspicions—if, that is, somebody happened to look. Margolies found another way. On his return from Florida, a friend introduced him to an Israeli diamond merchant named Zvi Oxenberg. Oxenberg was in New York on behalf of Bitterman Diamond of Israel trying to make a distress sale of some very good diamonds. They were valued at $180,000 on the market, and he was willing to part with them for $122,000. When he learned that Margolies owned Candor Diamond and so was in the business, he offered him the gems. It was such a good deal that Margolies could not resist. But, he told Oxenberg, Candor really wasn't the right company to buy them, since its diamonds were not of such good quality. (Actually, there was another reason why Margolies decided not to buy through Candor. Had he done so, the diamonds would have become part of the Candor inventory, and Maguire had a security interest in that inventory.) Instead, he said, he would purchase them through M & M Merchandising. It was a company owned by his in-laws and he had an interest in it, he explained, and its credit was sterling. It would be the right vehicle to take on the stones. Then, using all his salesman's winning ways, Margolies managed to convince the Israeli not only to turn over the stones to him and M & M Merchandising, but also to wait until September 1, 1981, for payment and not to expect any interest.

The diamonds in his possession, Margolies moved to cash in on them. He hurried to his friend and independent auditor Harris Freedman and told Freedman he had just come into some precious gems. He offered to turn them over to Freedman at a distress price of $125,000 if Freedman would share the profits from their resale with him. Freedman agreed. To make the purchase from Margolies and then to handle the sale, which Margolies would assist with, Freedman set up a company called Gortz, Inc. And who was named president of Gortz? Madeleine Margolies. According to Freedman, she was given the post at the urging of Irwin Margolies. He said that if he was going to assist in selling the diamonds at their full value, or close to it, this would give him a certain credibility. He would be able to tell anyone who asked that the reason he was the one selling the diamonds for Gortz was because Gortz was his wife's company.

By early April, Gortz was in business. Freedman handed Margolies a check on the new company's account for $125,000, made out to the purported owner of the diamonds, M & M Merchandising. Margolies sent the check to his in-laws, the Malens. They deposited it in a sixty-day time account at a Florida bank. The maturity date on the account, as it happened, neatly coincided with the closing date on the Margolieses's Florida condominium. Indeed, as soon as the account matured, the bank issued a teller's check for the $125,000, payable to Madeleine Margolies. She endorsed it over to the seller of the condominium. But with that check and the 10 percent down payment, the Margolieses still were $12,250 short of the full purchase price. Again, no problem. On the day of the closing, Herman Malen visited three different Florida banks, his pockets stuffed with cash, and came away with bank checks for the necessary balance.

The closing was held, the money changed hands, and the

condominium belonged to the Margolieses. They took steps to make sure that it continued to belong to them no matter what later ensued. They told the seller to hold on to the title for the next several months before filing it. And when it finally was filed, showing that the condominium belonged to Madeleine Margolies, another document also was recorded showing that the property was mortgaged for $125,000 and that the holder of the mortgage was M & M Merchandising. It was a very unusual mortgage. First of all, no interest was payable on it. And even more unusual, the mortgage matured and became payable only when and if the condominium ever was sold. If, however, Madeleine Margolies decided that she wanted to transfer the ownership as, say, a gift to her husband, Irwin, or to her sons, Stephen and Douglas, or to her brother, Scott Malen, or to her parents, Herman and Molly Malen, or to anyone else, the mortgage would remain intact and not have to be paid off.

Meanwhile, there were the Oxenberg diamonds, now owned by Gortz. At about the time of the closing on the condominium in Florida, Irwin Margolies sent his brother-in-law, Scott Malen, around to see Harris Freedman. Margolies had little use for Malen other than as a messenger boy, though he employed him as a salesman for Candor. "He's a schmuck," Margolies complained to his lawyer, Oestericher, and to others, "but what can I do? He's my brother-in-law." Malen arrived at Freedman's office bearing a note from Margolies. The note asked Freedman to turn over the Oxenberg diamonds to Malen, who would, in turn, deliver them to Margolies. The jeweler explained that he needed physical possession of them because he was about to make a selling trip to show them to prospective buyers. Freedman complied. Malen took the diamonds and handed them to Margolies. Freedman never saw them again, and he never saw any money, and he was out the $125,000 that he, and Gortz, had paid for them. September 1 came and went and no money was paid by M & M Merchandising or anyone else to Zvi Oxenberg for the diamonds. His distress sale had, indeed, been a distress, for him and his principal in Israel, Bitterman Diamond.

Diamonds, of course, were an obsession with Margolies.

They were his hedge against the future, whatever it might bring, they would see him through anything. Accumulating diamonds, then, was his passion. By early summer of 1981, he had the Oxenberg diamonds and he had the diamonds he had swindled from Van Mopes. And he had a lot more. He was pouring Maguire money into the purchase of diamonds, and not the low-quality stones that Candor used to make its merchandise, but very high-quality gems. The money to buy those diamonds—and here he was buying and not attempting to swindle anyone but Maguire—from the best suppliers was channeled through Candor, which had no use for them, and through a new company, Madeleine Chain Corporation, set up in April 1981 with Madeleine Margolies as president and her brother, Scott Malen, as vice-president, theoretically to make and sell low-quality, low-cost trinkets. Between them, Candor and Madeleine Chain bought $2,250,000 worth of the best diamonds by the summer of 1981.

And what happened to those diamonds? In the spring of 1981, one day Scott Malen was hanging around the Candor-Madeleine Chain offices on West Forty-seventh Street when his sister summoned him. She had a bag on her desk that she could hardly lift. She asked Malen to carry it for her. Together they made their way down the street to a nearby branch of Manufacturers Hanover Trust Company and down to the safe-deposit area. Madeleine Margolies signed the register for a safe-deposit box rented by a company called A & B Amusement Corp. It was a dummy, of course. It had just been formed. Its officers on the corporate register were listed as Samuel, Molly, and Ann Tuttleman. Molly Malen's maiden name was Molly Tuttleman. And the offices of A & B Amusement were the same as those occupied by the Margolieses's friend and attorney Henry Oestericher. At the bank's vault, Madeleine Margolies took the heavy, bulging bag from her brother and disappeared into the safe-deposit area, along with a safety-deposit box measuring nearly two feet by two feet by two feet. A little later, she reappeared with the bag and handed it back to Malen. It was now empty. (Two years later, the FBI obtained a search warrant and went into that box. It recovered four hundred diamonds worth about $600,000. That is about all that has ever been recovered of the $2,250,000 in diamonds purchased by Margolies and the other $3 million swindled from Maguire.)

But the diamonds in the safety-deposit box at Manufacturers Hanover and in other safety-deposit boxes in other banks, in the United States and abroad, were only part of the horde. Another part was put into the hands of a jeweler friend on Forty-seventh Street, Josef Gubits, to hold for safekeeping and, if necessity dictated, to turn quickly into cash.

But in his own amassing of great wealth and turning it to his own purposes, Irwin Margolies did not forget Margaret Barbera, who kept his books and who advised him and showed him ways to work his scheme so it would not be detected. She had been hired in June as a part-time bookkeeper. By September 1980, she was the full-time comptroller of Candor, keeper of the several sets of books and accounts and of its secrets. And her salary was $32,000 a year. But that wasn't enough, not with all the Margolieses were getting away with. She thought she deserved more. Margolies complied. He doubled her salary.

The Margolieses were buying cars every time she turned around. Barbera thought she ought to have a car, too, and she told Irwin Margolies so. He bought her a BMW.

She had a very close friend, Jenny Soo Chin, who was getting bored with life as a housewife. Besides, they were such close friends that they wanted to spend as much time together as they could. Barbera told Margolies she needed an assistant, and she wanted him to hire Jenny Soo Chin as that assistant. Margolies offered no argument. He hired Chin.

After a few months, Barbera told Margolies that she was working so hard, she needed a vacation. She and Chin would just love to go to Europe for a few weeks. Margolies agreed that she deserved that vacation and, what's more, he would foot the tab for that European vacation for her and Chin. And he did it not once but twice. (There is some speculation, but no hard evidence, that on those European trips, Barbera and Chin did more than play. The theory goes that she carried with her cash and diamonds, that she deposited them in safe-deposit boxes and secret numbered accounts, and that if some of those boxes and accounts belonged to Margolies, others belonged to her, and that what she put there will now remain unclaimed.)

One thing she hated, she told Margolies, was regular office hours, a nine-to-five job. Besides, the kind of work she was doing for him was not something she, or he, wanted done when there were other people around with prying eyes. He complied. She could set her own hours. She did, often arriving for work just as everyone was leaving, and working long into the night, often arriving for work on Saturday and Sunday when the office was otherwise empty, unless, of course, there was special work to do. Margolies never complained. But, then, there was little for him to complain about. Barbera was everything he had hoped for when he hired her, and more.

And so anything Barbera wanted, Margolies granted, within reason. But, with it all, with all of Margolies's compliance with her every wish, she never completely trusted him, no more than he completely trusted her. She took steps to protect herself should she need protection. She took sets of the Candor books and ledgers home and secreted them in her cluttered closet, and she let Margolies know that she had them.

Margolies always had intended that when and if his scheme collapsed, it would be Barbera, not he and Madeleine, who would take the fall. Barbera would be his patsy. Perhaps it was her revelation that she had in her possession the records that would clearly show just what had been done and how, that would shift at least part, and the major part, of the responsibility back to Margolies, that told him it was time to set his plan in motion.

12

One day in early May 1981, Margolies summoned Oestericher. According to Oestericher, if he can be believed, while he was always aware of the general outlines of the Margolies swindle, at that moment he was not cognizant of the details or the scope. But he knew enough to realize how successful Margolies's plan had become. It was his hope and dream that soon, very soon, Margolies would offer him that implied partnership in a jewelry business, one that would make him rich and independent. And so anything that his friend wanted him to do, he was willing to do.

On that May day, Margolies wanted to talk about Barbera. She was doing a good job, he admitted. But she was untrustworthy. She had made off with copies of the books and records. It was essential to get them back and, at the same time, cast a cloud of suspicion over her, that she was not the loyal employee she seemed but a devious and possibly dishonest person who was stealing from Candor and trying to cover her tracks.

What Margolies wanted was Oestericher's help in manufacturing some sort of evidence to show that Barbera must be stealing from Candor, and then he wanted to hire a private detective who would be given the evidence and who would then, among other things, shadow her for a time, thereby implying that Margolies was very concerned that his comptroller was not all she seemed.

He and Oestericher discussed the first phase and came up with what they were sure was an ideal solution. They got a copy, easily obtained, of a Merrill Lynch transaction slip and filled it in. It revealed that on November 13, 1980, Margaret Barbera had purchased 4,325 shares of Superior Oil Company of Nevada for $795,800. Copies of the document were made, ready for whatever use Margolies wanted to make of them. (As it happened, Barbera did maintain an account with Merrill Lynch and, indeed, had used it at one time to purchase on margin shares in Superior Oil, but her holdings had never exceeded $21,000.)

Then they hired a private investigator named Linwood Lewis, handed him a copy of the phony stock transaction slip, and set him to work. He looked into Barbera's background and followed her for a couple of weeks, handed in a report, and then was told that his services were no longer required.

Lewis's report stated, "On May 21, 1981, an investigation was started to monitor the movements of Ms Barbera when she was not at work at 15 West 47th St., N.Y.C. The purpose was to find out if she was working at another job, or to find out the reason why she did not work a 9 to 5 job like most people."

On at least a dozen occasions, Lewis tailed her. He noted, "On May 29, 1981, around 11:30 P.M., upon arriving at 15 West 47th St., I observed lights on the entire floor. Subject left the building around 2:15 A.M. She walked up 45th St. to Fifth Ave., down Fifth Ave. to 44th St. and disappeared in the garage on 44th St. between Fifth and Sixth Ave. Upon entering the garage after waiting outside for her, she could not be found. Asked the attendant, he stated he saw no one, but that there is another exit. One exit is on 44th St. and one on 43rd St. Checked with

96

the cashier. She knew who I was talking about, because she stated she sees the lady and the car around this time a few times a week. She said the lady had just left. On my daytime surveillance, the subject would either go shopping at A. & S. and Macy's on Queens Blvd. or just stay at home. Twice I followed her on the weekend to her girlfriend's home in Teaneck, New Jersey. Learned from subject's neighbors that she is a very quiet person and she stays to herself. About visitors, it was learned that a Chinese woman comes to visit, but that's just about it. On the nights that I have followed her home from 45th St., she has gone directly home. She is not one of the slowest drivers in the world. Once she leaves the Midtown Tunnel exit on the Queens side of the tunnel, she runs like a bat out of hell. She opens up that BMW."

Checking on Barbera's background, Lewis found that until she went to work for Margolies, she had been something of a deadbeat. She had once had an account at Abraham & Straus department store, while she was in college, but she had fallen behind and it had been turned over for collection. The same thing had happened with a charge account at J. C. Penney, and a $1,262 loan she had taken out at Chemical Bank also was in default. She had borrowed money from the United Student Aid Fund to pay her tuition at NYU, and that had never been repaid. At about the same period, she had borrowed from Beneficial Finance Company to buy a 1971 Chevrolet, had neglected to pay the last $45 on the loan, and that, too, had been turned over to the lawyers for collection.

But then, suddenly, she seemed to have plenty of money. She had bought a 1981 BMW 320i and paid the $17,700 purchase price with a cashier's check, and then came up with another couple of hunded dollars for some extras. The BMW, Lewis noted, was registered in New Jersey at an address in Teaneck, the home of Edward and Jenny Soo Chin, who other than being Barbera's assistant at Candor and her very close friend and frequent companion "does little else but watch her children."

In sum, Lewis concluded, there was nothing to point to her

having committed any criminal acts. The only suspicious facts he could find was where she had come up with the money to pay for the BMW and where she kept her money, since she kept nothing in New York State, perhaps because she owed money in the state. But that was all.

There was, though, something else that Margolies and Oestericher asked Lewis to do. They asked him to break into Barbera's apartment and search it. Margolies was sure she had books and records of Candor somewhere in that apartment, he told Lewis, and they didn't belong to her, she had stolen them, and he wanted them back. Lewis was appalled. He wouldn't hear of doing such a thing. He had a license and Margolies was asking him to commit a criminal act that, if discovered, would cost him that license and drive him out of his profession.

If Margolies was disappointed that Lewis would not do this bidding, still, the private detective had served a purpose. He had noted a few strange things about Barbera and her behavior, and he knew that Margolies was concerned about her and about her honesty and loyalty. Thus, should Margolies ever need a witness to testify that, as early as the spring of 1981 if not before, Irwin Margolies had been suspicious of his comptroller, he had one.

So Margolies, with Oestericher's help, was weaving a web to entrap Barbera. He had what he thought was solid evidence—on the surface, anyway—in the form of the Merrill Lynch slip, that Barbera had made away with nearly $800,000. He had Lewis's report and Lewis's memory of what he had seen and been told. And there was more. In the spring of 1981, the diamonds turned over to Margolies and Candor by Van Mopes had disappeared, and so had the diamonds turned over to Margolies by Oxenberg. Margolies was concocting evidence to show that it was not he but Margaret Barbera who had made away with them, and not only them but also Candor's entire inventory of diamonds, worth, he would claim, about $2.5 million, and she was holding them for ransom, demanding an immediate payment of $100,000 in cash for their return.

So Margolies was prepared to turn all the blame for all that had happened, to Maguire and everyone else, on Barbera. He was sure he had covered every aspect, that nothing could touch him. It was not that he expected his scheme to tumble yet. He thought it still had a long way to go before anyone caught on, and that there still were millions more to be made.

And, then, suddenly, it all collapsed.

13

One hot evening late in the spring of 1981, two old acquaintances ran into each other at a cocktail party in Westchester County. One was an executive of John P. Maguire and the other an executive from the Zayre department store chain. They had known each other socially for years, and they often had met at such parties, since they had many mutual friends. They had not, of course, ever done any business together, Zayre not being in the habit of turning to factors for its short-term money, and Maguire not supplying funds to the retail industry nor, as it happened, having manufacturing clients who sold to Zayre.

Sometime in the middle of that evening, the two found themselves alone in the middle of the crowd. There were some pleasantries, inconsequential conversation, and then the man from Maguire commented lightly that maybe one of these days they ought to have lunch in town to celebrate the fact that finally they were doing some business together.

The man from Zayre looked blank. He wasn't aware, he

said, that Zayre had turned to Maguire for some factoring money, or that Maguire had moved into the retail financing business.

The man from Maguire laughed. That wasn't what he meant, of course, he said. What he meant was that Zayre was buying a lot of jewelry from Candor Diamond and that Maguire was factoring Candor's sales, so in that way, at least, they were obviously on a business footing these days.

The man from Zayre still looked blank. The name Candor Diamond rang no bells with him.

Well, the man from Maguire said, he guessed people don't always know what other people in the same company are up to.

The conversation went on to other things then. But the man from Zayre kept thinking through the weekend about what his friend had said. There was something troubling about it. If one of Zayre's suppliers was factoring its sales, which meant that Zayre would be sending checks to the factor, he was in a position to know. And he knew nothing, could remember nothing about sending any checks to Maguire, could remember nothing about a company called Candor Diamond.

Back in the office on Monday, he did a little checking, then called his friend from Maguire. I think somebody's putting one over on you, he said. I've looked at the records. Zayre did a little buying from this company, Candor Diamond, a couple of years ago. We took about two thousand dollars' worth of their stuff. There wasn't much demand for the jewelry and it didn't sell very well, so that was the end of it. We haven't bought anything from them since.

That was very disturbing news, indeed. Candor had filed a number of invoices with Maguire showing very large sales and shipments to Zayre, had just filed another one declaring it had sold and shipped $124,000 worth of merchandise to the chain, and Maguire had deposited the required $105,400 in Candor's account.

The worried executive went to W. H. Casey, who recently had succeeded Peter O'Neill as the Maguire official in charge of the Candor account. What to do? A look through the records

101

revealed that by that date, Candor was into Maguire for nearly $5.5 million that remained outstanding and unpaid. If Margolies was pulling a fraud, which it certainly looked as though he was, then Maguire was in very serious trouble. It could, of course, move rapidly and try to seize the Candor inventory of diamonds, which Margolies had given the factor a lien on and that the jeweler had said was worth $2.5 million. But that still would leave another $3 million owing. That was just too big a loss to swallow. Perhaps, Casey and others at Maguire, with whom he discussed the troubling situation, reasoned, a little quiet pressure might set things aright, might salvage something.

Another Maguire executive had a friend who was an FBI agent assigned to the New Rochelle office in Westchester. He called his friend and explained the problem and the growing suspicions that Margolies had perpetrated a major fraud. The agent listened. Did Maguire want to press federal fraud charges? Not at the moment, the Maguire executive said. What the factor wanted was its money back, or at least as much of it as it could get. Maybe a little quiet investigation to see if, indeed, Margolies had committed a fraud, and if that turned up, then maybe a semi-official call to Margolies to tell him that the game was up, that all was known, that he was, at the moment, facing the possibility of a civil action, but that if he made good on what he owed Maguire, then perhaps no criminal action would follow and the whole thing would just fade away.

It didn't take long for the agent to discover that the feared fraud had taken place, though its dimensions still were unclear. But the call to Margolies resulted only in denial, only in Margolies's claim that he didn't know what the agent was talking about. And it did something else: It alerted Margolies. He knew now that the scheme was coming apart.

He got further evidence of that a few days later, in mid-June. Casey called. Maguire, he said, had been marveling at the miraculous growth in Candor's sales in the past few months. It was so miraculous that he wanted to bring a team of auditors into Candor's offices and go over the books.

When? Margolies asked.

He'd like to do it right away, Casey said. But, unfortunately, that wouldn't be possible. He and an important member of the audit team were about to go on a month-long vacation. They wouldn't be back until the middle of July. How about then?

Fine, Margolies said.

That gave Margolies another month, and he made the most of it. Invoices, claiming millions of dollars in sales and shipments, poured out of Candor's offices and into Maguire. And within a week of that call from Casey, announcing the impending audit, Irwin and Madeleine Margolies applied for United States passports on an expedited basis. They claimed they had reservations for a flight to Israel in June. Actually, their travel plans, which were made only after the Casey call, scheduled them to leave for Tel Aviv on August 9. But they wanted those passports, and they wanted them as quickly as possible, ready for use in case of an emergency. They did more. They prepared for what might turn out to be a lengthy stay abroad. They prepaid three months of installments on the mortgage on their Westchester home. They paid notes given for the purchase of high-quality diamonds, notes that were not due for several months. They somehow managed to persuade Candor's few legitimate customers, among them Caldor and the Army-Air Force Exchange Service, who knew of the factoring agreement with Maguire and had been paying the factor as required, to skip that step and pay their bills directly to Candor, which enriched them by another $100,000. And they began to siphon off more money and transfer it out of the United States, perhaps to enable them to live in the style to which they were growing accustomed. Through Bank Leumi in New York, Margolies opened a personal account at Bank Leumi Israel in Tel Aviv and then, between June 19 and July 23, he transferred $200,000 out of Candor's New York account into that new personal one in Israel.

Then Casey was back from vacation. On July 24, first thing in the morning, he called Margolies to invite him to lunch, not just with Casey but also with Casey's superior, James Amato. It was hardly an invitation. It was an order. Margolies arrived.

Casey and Amato told him that the audit was going to take place immediately. Margolies balked. That was impossible, he declared. The jewelry show was taking place over the weekend and into the following week. Everybody at Candor would be involved, and so nobody would be available to assist the Maguire auditors. They could come in sometime later the following week and go over the books, and they would have complete cooperation. Then Margolies turned back into his affable self. He invited Casey and Amato to visit the Candor display at the New York Hilton during the show and take a look at just how good the line was. Were they interested? They were. Fine, Margolies said, he would call and set a convenient time for the visit. Then, lunch finished, he departed, saying he would be in touch with Casey very soon.

That night, Margaret Barbera went looking for Margolies. She had important things to discuss with him if they were to be prepared fully for the impending Maguire audit. She went to the Hilton, to the Candor booth. Margolies was not there. She went down to the Candor offices on Forty-seventh Street. When she reached the office doors, she could hear a lot of noise from inside, the sound of things being moved around, loud voices, perhaps an argument of some kind. She couldn't be sure. But when she tried to enter, Scott Malen barred the way. She was not permitted into the offices, he told her. Why not? she asked. It was vital that she see Margolies without delay. Impossible, Malen told her. Margolies himself had given specific instructions that she was to be kept out. Barbera turned and went home.

On Monday morning, July 27, Margolies called his travel agency. He and Madeleine, he said, had to leave for Israel right away. They couldn't wait until August 9, when they were supposed to leave. Was there a flight that day? If so, they had to be on it. The travel agency checked. There were seats available on a TWA flight leaving that evening. Book them, Margolies ordered.

Before he and Madeleine departed for the airport, he went to Bank Leumi and cashed a check for $15,000. And then he wrote two more checks, for $25,000 each, to Oestericher and Oestericher's law partner, Norman Schwartz, and delivered them. The checks were for legal services, already rendered and to be rendered.

And then they were off.

Through the weekend, Casey waited for Margolies to call to set up the visit to the jewelry show. The call did not come. Monday passed and still he did not hear from his client. On Tuesday morning, he called Candor's office and spoke to Thelma Williams, the receptionist. He told her he had been expecting a call from Margolies but it had not come, and he was wondering just when he could go up to the Hilton to see the Candor exhibit. Williams said Margolies was traveling and she had not heard from him for several days, but someone would get back to Casey.

No one got back to Casey. He called Candor again on Wednesday and again on Thursday, and got the same response from the receptionist. He began to get very worried. On Friday, July 31, he called Harris Freedman, Candor's accountant and, though Casey didn't know it, Margolies's partner in Gortz, Inc. He told Freedman that over the past couple of months, Maguire had been receiving an assignment of about $500,000 a week in Candor sales and had been depositing about $450,000 every week in Candor's bank account. Suddenly it had stopped. Over the past week, he said, there had been no assignment of sales and no requests for advances. What's up? he asked. Freedman had no idea. Could Freedman check, Casey asked, since he had been unable to locate Margolies all week? Freedman agreed.

Later in the day, Freedman called Casey. He had called the Margolies home in Westchester, he reported, and had spoken to Madeleine's parents, Herman and Molly Malen. They told him they had no idea where Irwin and Madeleine were and that they were staying at the house to take care of the two boys.

Casey immediately called Candor again. Once more, Thelma Williams told him that Margolies was away. But this time she said that his brother-in-law, Scott Malen, was in charge. He asked whether she knew if there would be any sales assignments for that week. She didn't know, and then she asked if Maguire was going to make an advance so Candor could meet its payroll.

Casey was a very worried man. He decided it was time to do some very close checking. He ordered his collection department to begin trying to verify the nearly $6 million in accounts receivable assigned by Candor to Maguire.

Over the next twenty-four hours, Carlos Paniagua, Maguire's collection manager, made thirteen calls to thirteen supposed Candor customers. All but two denied they had ever bought or received or been billed for any Candor merchandise. The two exceptions were Caldor and the Army-Air Force Exchange Service. And Caldor said yes, they had bought Candor jewelry, about $3,500 worth, but that the money had not been paid, since it went against a $31,716 debt owed to it by Candor. According to the invoices assigned by Candor to Maguire, Caldor had purchased $415,000 worth of trinkets during that period.

Over the same period, Paniagua's next in command, Peter Paul Petraglia, called sixteen other supposed Candor customers. Every one of them denied having any record of open accounts with Candor, though a few said that in the past they had bought jewelry from the manufacturer, but not in the amounts Petraglia questioned them about. On his books, for example, Helzberg's Diamonds in Kansas City owed Candor, and thus Maguire, $342,000. On Helzberg's books, the amount bought from Candor during all of 1981 was only $32,000, and that had long since been paid.

Casey was staggered. It now looked as though nearly every assignment of sales by Candor to Maguire had been a fiction, and Maguire had advanced millions against nothing. He called Harris Freedman and broke the news to him. Freedman said he was thunderstruck. When Casey asked, Freedman agreed to go with the Maguire official to Candor's offices, look at the books and records, and check to make sure that the gold and diamond inventory was intact, was worth the more than the $2.5 million that Margolies had claimed in his agreement with Maguire, giving Maguire a security interest in that stock.

106

On the afternoon of August 7, Casey, Freedman, and one of Freedman's associates made the trip to Forty-seventh Street. They were greeted by the receptionist, Thelma Williams. They told her they had come to examine the books and records and take a physical audit of the inventory. She told them Malen was away, at the bank, and she could not let them in.

Later, two more Maguire officials made the journey to Forty-seventh Street. They, too, were blocked at the door. Casey called the office, spoke once more to Williams, asked again if he could come to Candor. Once more she told him Malen was not in and she could do nothing without his permission. Casey asked if Candor intended to assign any more sales or request any more advances. Williams said she didn't know. And then, just before the conversation ended, she asked, plaintively, if she was going to be paid that week.

Maguire officials now summoned their attorney, David Blejwas of Hahn and Hessen, for advice. When Blejwas heard what they had turned up—that about 80% of all the invoices assigned to Maguire for payment since the beginning of the factoring agreement were phony, and that nearly all of those submitted since April 1981, on which more than $5 million had been advanced, had no basis in reality—he said that the only answer was to throw Candor into bankruptcy and thus try to save what could be saved, if anything. On August 10, Blejwas went into Bankruptcy Court and made his arguments, won his point, and obtained an order declaring Candor involuntarily bankrupt. The court then authorized an interim trustee and a federal marshal to enter Candor's premises, by force if necessary, and seize the company's assets.

Before the day was out, the trustee, the marshal, and Maguire representatives were in the Forty-seventh Street offices. They searched every corner. They went through the inventory and what books they could find. When they left, they were filled with disbelief and shock. The inventory was practically non-existent. There was only about $10,000 worth of jewelry. Half the books were missing. And the bank records revealed that Candor's account stood at $52,000.

PART
THREE

DEALS

14

They were no innocents abroad, taking in the sights and sounds
of the Holy Land and the Old World with wide-eyed incredulity.
Irwin Margolies later would say that the trip was a long-planned
vacation, not a hurried flight, that it was a needed respite from
the incredible pressures of his hectic business, and that it was
also an attempt to combine a little business with some deserved
pleasure, to renew old contacts and make new ones, to find
sources for the materials he needed to make his jewelry, to sell
his merchandise in new markets, and to settle some business
problems. He and his wife, he would say, had not traveled in
high style. Far from it. They had actually lived on the edge of
penury while abroad. To pay for the trip and to pay off some
outstanding business obligations, he had been forced to sell
Madeleine's engagement ring, earrings, and other jewelry within
days of their arrival in Israel.

It made a nice story. It had about the same elements and
ring of truth as most of his other tales. And it would have

amazed the manager of Bank Leumi Israel on Ben-Yehuda Street in Tel Aviv had he heard it, for two days after their arrival, Irwin and Madeleine Margolies appeared in his office. After long discussion and explanations, they opened a secret numbered account. It was in both their names, jointly. Only the bank manager had access to the records revealing their identities. No correspondence relating to the account was to be mailed to the United States. They opened the account with $200,000, in a three-month certificate of deposit earning 19% interest. (Margolies later would claim that the $200,000 had been withdrawn from Candor's New York account and transferred to Israel in the first place to help cover his business debts and that it had been almost immediately withdrawn after the deposit for just that purpose. Abiding by the country's banking regulations, Bank Leumi Israel kept its silence.)

The couple stayed in Israel for two weeks, touring, seeing the sights, and doing a little business in that very important center of the world diamond industry. Then it was on to Munich, where they rented a car for a drive to Zurich. That city is, of course, home to most of Switzerland's major banks and the center of the fabled secret numbered account. By the time the Margolieses departed Zurich, they had a few, and Madeleine had a new $1,100 mink jacket to console her for the supposed sale of her jewelry in Israel.

Then it was back across the Atlantic, not home yet but to Canada. In Toronto, they rented a car to drive across the border to Detroit. In Detroit, they assumed false names and under them boarded a plane for Florida.

While they were away, though, they were not cut off from events at home, not ignorant of what was going on, not out of touch at all. Margolies called Oestericher almost every day, at his office and at home, held lengthy conversations in which he was completely filled in and during which he gave explicit instructions to be carried out in his absence. And he and Madeleine spoke often with their sons, Steven and Douglas, though never over the phone to their home in Greenburgh. Oestericher made the arrangements. Steven and Douglas were to go to

112

specified public phone booths at appointed hours and a call would come to that phone from their parents, wherever they happened to be.

There was much that Oestericher and the Margolies sons had to report, and much that Margolies had to tell them, especially Oestericher. Candor might now be dead, or on its deathbed, bled of every ounce of vitality and viability, but in its place stood Madeleine Chain. In the absence of Margolies, it was being run by Madeleine's brother, Scott Malen, as quondam president and owner, Madeleine later claiming that she had sold him all the stock for a few thousand dollars. Margolies hardly trusted Malen to run even the simplest errands let alone to guide the destiny of a company that he felt was crucial to his future plans. Through Oestericher Margolies gave the directives that guided Malen in his operations.

As important as anything to Margolies was to keep track of Barbera, not to let her feel abandoned in this crisis. Though Madeleine Chain had no offices and no sales, it did maintain desk space at Oestericher's office. And Malen was instructed to keep three of Candor's employees and to pay them in cash every week. Those three included a diamond sorter, the Candor office manager, and Margaret Barbera.

But Madeleine Chain served other purposes, too. It was a funnel through which laundered Candor-Maguire money could be channeled to the Margolieses for their own uses. For instance, Madeleine Chain, according to its books, was kept afloat for a time through an advance of $30,000 from a man named Boaz Sussman. Malen said the money had been received in cash in three separate parcels delivered by the postman. Sussman, however, had a different story when he was turned up. It seems that he was a distant relative of Oestericher and, at Oestericher's urgent entreaties, he had loaned Madeleine Chain about $2,000. And that was the extent of his involvement.

By mid-September, Irwin and Madeleine Margolies were home. The FBI, among others, very much wanted to talk to them, and especially Irwin. What had been a semi-official investigation had, with the uncovering of the fraud and the action to throw Candor into involuntary bankruptcy early in August, become official. The case was on the desk of Special Agent Robert Paquette, working out of the New Rochelle office. He meticulously went through all the records and files and books he could find of Candor and its customers, real and fictional, and of Maguire, and confirmed all that Maguire had feared. What he wanted then was very much to talk to Irwin Margolies. But Margolies was nowhere to be found.

Then he surfaced and called the FBI and said, in all innocence, that he understood somebody wanted to talk to him. An appointment was made for him to appear at the U.S. attorney's office on the morning of September 23. With him was his attorney, Henry Oestericher. Margolies was at his most winning and cooperative, and injured. He answered every question, had explanations for every seeming contradiction and problem. The trip to Israel and the transfer of the $200,000 from New York to Tel Aviv? Simple. The trip was a vacation; the transfer was money to pay business obligations; there had been no luxury journey, though; he and his wife were so broke on that trip that he had to pawn her jewels to raise the cash to finance it.

The swindle of Maguire? He was completely unaware of that until it had all come down around his head. It was all the doing of his comptroller, Margaret Barbera. He had so trusted her that he had given her complete control over the company's books and records, had permitted her to handle the assignments to the factor and all the rest. And now look how she had betrayed him. She had done it to enrich herself. She had destroyed him and his company in the process. She had put him in this kind of jeopardy. His trust had been misplaced. Obviously she was an evil, greedy person, and the law ought to come down on her.

Did the authorities want to know what she had done? He would tell them, at least as much as he knew, and he was sure there was much more that he didn't know. For one thing, she had used a lot of the money she had stolen from him, and Maguire, to make investments for her own personal aggran-

114

dizement. And here, he and Oestericher produced the Merrill Lynch order slip showing the purchase of about $795,000 worth of Superior Oil stock. Where had they found that slip? Why, just before Irwin and Madeleine left for Israel, they had searched Barbera's desk and, lo and behold, there it was.

And just why had they happened to have searched the desk of Barbera, until then the person they considered a loyal employee, until then the person they relied on so completely, until then considered their regent in their absence? Why, because on July 27, as they were getting ready to leave for Israel, she had called Irwin and told him that she had taken the entire inventory of diamonds and gold and hidden it and would not return it unless Margolies paid her $100,000, and she wanted it without delay, immediately, not after their return from their trip. And, Margolies said, Oestericher could confirm this. He had called Oestericher as soon as he got that message from Barbera and told him about it. Oestericher confirmed it.

So the FBI talked to Barbera. She didn't know what they were talking about. All she was was a bookkeeper, with the glorified title of comptroller. All she did was keep the books. All she did was write down what Irwin and Madeleine Margolies told her to write down. She wasn't supposed to ask any questions, and she didn't. She had never bought $800,000 worth of stocks in her life. She had never stolen any jewelry from Candor and held it for ransom. Obviously Margolies was lying about her to cover up for what he had done. She was not a thief and had never been one. She'd had nothing to do with the fraud that had taken place. That was all the doing of Irwin and Madeleine Margolies and she wasn't even aware of it, she had never questioned the figures they had given her, had always thought they must be correct. It was a terrible thing to have loyalty, and she had given them her complete loyalty, rewarded this way.

It was, for the moment, a standoff. Margolies was claiming loudly that he was innocent, he was wronged, it was all Barbera's doing, and Barbera was saying that she was innocent, she had done nothing, she was the wronged party, and she was pointing her finger at Margolies. Paquette and the other FBI agents now on the case, and the lawyers in the U.S. attorney's office, might be fairly certain that Margolies was the guilty party, but belief is one thing and proof is another, and they didn't have the proof. It was Margolies's word against Barbera's. The authorities were sure, too, that Barbera knew a lot more than she was telling. If they could turn her, she might lead them to the convincing and convicting evidence that would wrap the net tightly around Margolies and, perhaps, get Maguire some if not all of its money back, which was, of course, what everyone wanted.

Barbera could have given them exactly what they wanted and needed. She had Candor's books, the ones that would reveal just what had been done to Maguire and how. And Margolies knew she had those books, knew that his future depended on what she did with them. In the fall of 1981, it was Barbera's intention to do precisely nothing with those books except sit on them. For one thing, they were, she thought, her protection against any retribution from her one-time employer and now her enemy, and having worked for and with him for so long, she knew that he was capable of many things. There were phone calls now, as the year was dying, threatening phone calls from Margolies. He ordered her to keep her mouth sealed. He ordered her to return the books. He threatened dire consequences if she should talk or if she didn't return those records, or if she should show them to anyone, especially those who were investigating the case.

She had no intention of doing any of those things. Her own safety, and not just from Margolies's wrath, depended on her silence and her resistance to any pressure, from any source. If she talked and turned those books over to Paquette or the federal lawyers, she was in very great danger from them. Those books would reveal just how deeply she was involved in the swindle, how great a role she had played in it, that she was not the innocent she claimed but a willing participant, if not as guilty as Margolies, nevertheless very guilty herself. So she kept her silence and she kept her distance and she held to her story. The authorities pressed. She held fast.

*   *   *

In those months, Margolies was putting several faces to the world. There was the sad, defeated face. He filed for personal bankruptcy. He was, he declared, without assets and a ruined man, all because he had trusted a woman not deserving of his trust.

There was the devious face, scheming to save what he had taken and ensure his future. With Maguire and all those other creditors closing in, the first thing was to save the Greenburgh house from their grasp. There was that $180,000 mortgage still outstanding with Scarsdale National Bank, and he was very worried about that. Scarsdale was a wholly owned subsidiary of Irving Trust Company. So was John P. Maguire. Margolies thought that because of the relationship, the bank might foreclose and sell the house to begin to repay the debt to Maguire. It was vital to prevent that.

Margolies called in Oestericher, and with him hatched a way out. Oestericher knew a New Jersey real-estate broker named Harry W. Fry. They were, if not friends, at least close acquaintances who had done business together in the past. Now Oestericher called Fry and asked if he happened to know anyone who might have some free money around to take over a large mortgage on a Westchester home. Fry made a few inquiries, and then, before he had time to follow up, Oestericher called again. Forget it, he said. We've found a foreign investor by the name of S. Nussbaum, who's willing to take the mortgage as an investment, since it will be for just a year and pay sixteen percent interest. What we'd like you to do is represent Nussbaum at the closing and then act as his collection agent. For that we'll pay you a seven-thousand-dollar fee.

The closing took place in Oestericher's office on October 24. Madeleine Margolies was there, and so was Fry, and so were Oestericher and his sometime partner, Norman Schwartz. Nussbaum was absent, but Oestericher had a letter from Nussbaum that he showed to Fry giving his consent to the proceedings. Madeleine Margolies handed Oestericher a check for $180,000 drawn on a Zurich bank and made out to her, supposedly from

Nussbaum. The mortgage papers were signed and executed. Madeleine handed Fry a check on her personal account for $1,800 as partial payment for his fee, with the balance to be paid later. It was, by Oestericher, in cash. Schwartz assured Fry he would take care of recording the mortgage.

That out of the way, Madeleine Margolies moved quickly to protect her home. Oestericher handed the check back to her. She endorsed it over to the Scarsdale National Bank as payment in full for the $180,000 outstanding on the mortgage. It was dispatched to the bank.

If the Margolieses thought they were now fully protected, that they had saved their home, they were wrong. The relationship between the Scarsdale bank, Irving Trust, and Maguire being what it was, Irving Trust was not long in learning about the payment through the endorsed Zurich check, and, naturally, Maguire heard the news, too. Maguire's attorney, David Blejwas, hurried to court. He demanded that the check not be honored until there was a hearing to decide whether the money actually belonged to this Mr. S. Nussbaum, whom apparently nobody had ever seen and whose existence was attested to only by the letter Oestericher had shown Fry, or if it was actually laundered Candor money that, thus, rightfully belonged to Maguire.

This was very bad news for Margolies, and the list of enemies accumulating within his mind now expanded to include Blejwas. Margolies was determined to forestall that court action, to overturn it. He and Oestericher rushed out to New Jersey, arriving late in the evening just as Fry was closing his office. They had an affidavit with them for him to sign. It asserted that Fry had, indeed, found a foreign investor and placed the mortgage with him, and so the $180,000 check did not represent funds put up by Irwin or Madeleine Margolies or Candor but was money put up by this Mr. Nussbaum. Somehow or other, Margolies and Oestericher persuaded Fry to sign the affidavit, and Oestericher's partner, Schwartz, notarized it.

Then came the court hearing on Blejwas's motion. It was a staggering blow to Margolies. Fry renounced the affidavit. He told the court that he had never found a foreign investor for

118

the mortgage and so had no basis on which to say whether or not the $180,000 check came from the Margolieses or Candor or anyone else. In fact, he said, he had even tried to find this S. Nussbaum, but all his efforts had been fruitless. After hearing Fry's story, the court declared that the $180,000 did not belong to Nussbaum, whoever he might be, but rather to Candor and thus was part of Candor's assets that belonged to Maguire and so could not be used to pay off the Margolieses' mortgage.

Margolies was not one to surrender easily. He searched for ways to overturn that judgment and thought he had found one. He came up with Joseph Gubits, a jeweler friend of his on Forty-seventh Street. He got Gubits to swear to an affidavit that he was actually the unnamed foreign investor in the mortgage and that somehow he had been persuaded to make a loan of $180,000 to a business acquaintance, S. Nussbaum, to fund that mortgage. But when the court summoned Gubits to testify to this, he failed to appear. And so the court's judgment that Maguire had a legal right to the $180,000 Zurich check stood.

Later, appearing before a grand jury, Gubits would be asked about the whole affair. "Mr. Gubits," the question was posed, "in the affidavit there is a reference to a hundred eighty thousand dollars, and the statement that you signed that the check represents 'my personal funds, none of the funds of this mortgage loan came from Madeleine Margolies, Irwin Margolies, Candor Diamond Corp., or any member of the Margolies family or Candor Diamond Corp.' Is that statement true?"

"I signed it," Gubits said.

"Is the statement true?"

"Yes, sure."

"Is the last half of the statement true?"

"I didn't pay any attention to the names, here, but . . ."

"The one hundred eighty thousand dollars represented your personal funds?"

"Yes, sure."

"Where did the money come from, the one hundred eighty thousand dollars? Barclays Bank?"

"No."

"Mizrachi Bank?"

"No."

"Where?"

"From sales, what I sold in Switzerland," Gubits said.

"When?"

"Over the eighties. 1980."

"You left Israel with eight thousand dollars, nine thousand dollars. Aside from the eight thousand dollars, nine thousand dollars in cash and your investment in Gem Electronics . . . it is your testimony that you lent that one hundred eighty thousand dollars to Madeleine and Irwin Margolies for a year?"

"Yes."

The grand jury indicted Gubits, charging that he "unlawfully, willfully, knowingly, and corruptly impeded and endeavored to influence, obstruct, and impede the due administration of justice."

All that took years, of course. And the delays served the Margolieses' purpose. They retained their home. They even, while in danger of losing it, continued to spend money, despite their supposed bankruptcy and poverty, in the grand manner to refurnish and redecorate it regularly.

15

It had been a very bad autumn for Irwin Margolies, perhaps the worst in his life. He had all those millions in diamonds squirreled away in safety-deposit boxes, with his friend Joseph Gubits, and elsewhere, and he had all those other millions hidden in secret numbered bank accounts and other safe places, but he had to be very careful how he used that money. People were watching, calculating, trying to trap him, the FBI agents, the government attorneys, the people from Maguire. Caution was the word; there would be time in the future. But Madeleine still was spending in the grand style, still redecorating and refurnishing the house, still buying cars, and even though she was paying cash for everything, it still worried him. He told his friend Oestericher that he wished she'd slow down, but who can make a woman listen?

They still had the house, but that was only because the courts took so long to decide anything, and there always were appeals and arguments and the rest of the legal rigamarole to keep delaying things for a long time. But all his attempts to get a firm hold, to take it free and clear, had come crashing. That Maguire lawyer, Blejwas, had moved quickly and stopped them from paying off the mortgage with the check from Zurich, and their attempts to get Fry to come to their aid had backfired.

There had been the ignominy of the bankruptcy hearings, of having to testify and have Madeleine testify that they were wiped out, that they were the victims of an ungrateful and disloyal employee. And now, in bankruptcy, there was danger of losing everything, the boat, the cars, everything.

There had been that confrontation with David Blejwas, when the lawyer had seemed to be offering him a way out. The whole situation could be resolved, Blejwas had said to him, "if you tell me what happened to the Candor inventory." Of course, Blejwas hadn't meant exactly that. What he'd meant was, return those diamonds and return most of the cash you got away with. But that would mean going back to square one, back to the way things were before the thing with Maguire started. There was no way he was going back to that situation, no way he was going to be poor again, reaching for the gold ring that always was just beyond his grasp. He had told Blejwas he didn't know where the inventory was. "It was all Margaret Barbera's fault," he said.

Blejwas hadn't believed him, had sighed and said, "Give me a break."

And he had retorted, "I'd like to break your legs." He knew Blejwas knew he meant it.

In fact, nobody believed him. They were all sure he was lying, and they were just waiting for him to make a mistake, just waiting to turn up something, like the books, so they could nail him, and nail Madeleine, too.

Worst of all, there was Margaret Barbera. She was holding the sword over his head, with those books she had hidden and with her knowledge of just how everything had been done. She wouldn't listen to his entreaties or his promises or his threats. And now he was hearing that the government was putting more and more pressure on her, and her dear friend Jenny Soo Chin, to tell all, to make a deal and tell all and wrap up Irwin Margolies

122

like a Christmas present. The most important thing, he was sure, was to stop that from happening. Something had to be done about Margaret Barbera.

At the beginning of December, Margolies sat down with Oestericher. They were seeing a lot of each other now, more than usual. Now that he no longer had his own office, he was using Oestericher's as his own, was giving out Oestericher's private unlisted office phone number as the way to contact him.

That day, Margolies began to talk about Barbera, the problem she was posing for him and his future. What he'd like to do, he said, was put the fear of God, or if not God, of Irwin Margolies into her so she would turn back those books and records and forget everything she knew.

Oestericher agreed that that might solve a lot of problems. Without those books and without Barbera's knowledge, the government would have a very hard time proving a criminal case against him, and Maguire would have the same difficulty in a civil suit. It would always be Margolies's word against Barbera's word.

In fact, Margolies said, Oestericher, with all his contacts in the lower levels of society, must know someone, the very person to put that fear into Barbera.

Knowing Margolies so well, Oestericher knew he was serious. He said he would do some checking around.

The place to look, Oestericher decided, was over on the West Side, close by the docks. As it happened, he managed a building there, on West Forty-fifth Street. The superintendent of that building was a man named Alberto Torres. They had known each other for years. Torres had worked for Oestericher in a housing development the lawyer managed in New Jersey, and he had worked for him as superintendent at several apartment buildings and hotels in Manhattan, including the notorious Somerset on Father Duffy Square, and now he was working for him again on Forty-fifth Street. Now Oestericher made the trip across town to see Torres. He had a friend who was having a problem, he told the super.

What kind of a problem? Torres asked.

His friend, Oestericher said, had an employee who was getting way out of line. His friend would like to have someone explain to his employee that what was going on didn't make good sense and that the employee ought to straighten out and get back into line. Did Torres happen to know someone who might be good at doing this kind of explaining?

Torres said he'd ask around and get back to Oestericher.

Torres had an old friend named Donald Nash, who used to be Donald Bowers, of the notorious West Side docks Bowers family, until he took his mother's maiden name as his own. He considered Nash a very nice friendly sort of man, a very good and astute mechanic and jack-of-all-trades. He did a lot of work for Torres and for other people in the neighborhood, repairing electrical fixtures, plumbing, just about anything anybody needed, and he almost never charged for the favors. He had grown up on the West Side and was very knowledgeable about who was who and who would do what. Though he had long since moved to Keansburg, N.J., with his common-law wife and her daughter, whom he adored and both considered and treated as his own, he was frequently around the docks and had not lost his contacts or his friendships. And, for Torres, he was an easy man to reach. He maintained a desk and a telephone in connection with a struggling electrical contracting business at the rear of Vinnie Russo's catering establishment, which happened to be on the ground floor of the building Oestericher managed and Torres took care of.

Nash was the youngest of nine children, his father a bedridden diabetic until his death early in 1952, when Nash was sixteen, and his mother a drunk. At about the time of his father's death, doing very poorly in school and with an I.Q. of 89, he dropped out, worked sporadically as an errand boy and a parking-lot attendant. Mostly he roamed the streets of the neighborhood with his friends, a rather distinctive figure, medium height and stocky, with a drooping, nearly blind right eye, and a crushed cheekbone beneath, the result of having been hit in the eye and face while playing stickball in the streets when he was twelve.

124

He had been in trouble only once with the police, in 1951, when he was picked up for a burglary, sent to juvenile court, and put on probation. Then, in the spring of 1952, he got into serious trouble. While riding the subway one evening, he said, a homosexual tried to pick him up. Nash rewarded the man by beating him severely and then making off with about $450 worth of cash and jewelry the man had on him. Flushed with triumph, he joined a couple of friends for a joyride in a stolen car. The cops picked him up. He was tried, convicted, and sentenced to three years at the New York State prison in Elmira. He was a good prisoner, remorseful, and anxious, parole reports said, to make a good adjustment on the outside and not get into trouble again. After eighteen months, he was released on parole.

In the years that followed, Nash worked off and on at various construction jobs, as a cabdriver, at just about anything he could find. Though he was good with his hands and had certain mechanical abilities, he never made much money, and sometimes he turned to extralegal activities to supplement his meager income. Though it would be a long time before he got a prison sentence again, he was arrested at least nine times through the years, for a variety of offenses that included burglary, forgery, grand and petty larceny; he was convicted and fined a couple of times and then released. Still, none of his crimes had been what anyone he grew up with would have considered major. He was, people who knew him said, just another guy trying to make out, always broke or close to it, always trying to do his best to keep a roof over his family's heads, food on the table, and clothes on everybody's back. If he sometimes did things he shouldn't have done to accomplish that, well, a lot of other guys he grew up with were doing the same or a lot worse, and besides, as far as anybody knew, he had never hurt anybody.

One day, soon after his conversation with Oestericher, Alberto Torres cornered Nash as he came into Russo's place and headed for his desk and telephone. Taking Nash off to the side for a private conversation, Torres related what Oestericher had told him and then asked Nash if Nash knew anybody who could

125

use a little muscle in a persuasive manner. Nash thought about it for a moment, asked what it would pay. Torres said he didn't know but he was sure the party who wanted the strong-arming done would make it worthwhile to whomever did it. Nash thought some more and then said he'd take care of it. Later, Torres said he thought Nash meant that he would look around among all the people he knew on the docks and find the right guy. He said he didn't at that moment think that Nash meant he would take care of it personally.

But that was precisely what Donald Nash meant. He was then very broke and very much in need of money. His step-daughter was pregnant, separated from her husband after a brief and very unhappy marriage, and so Nash felt himself responsible for seeing her through the pregnancy to the birth of the child he would consider his grandson or granddaughter. It would not be a cheap thing to do. But his construction and repair work was sporadic at best and not bringing in very much, especially since he constantly charged less than the going rates if he thought his customer couldn't afford higher prices, and often he did the work as a favor. He was constantly borrowing from his nephew, Thomas Dane, who lived close by him in Keansburg, but Dane had only so much to lend.

So desperate had Nash been that a month before Torres cornered him, he had tried a little scam he had attempted a few years earlier and that had backfired then, leading to an arrest and $200 fine. From experience, he knew that cabdrivers could turn a nice living, especially if they owned their own cabs. But a medallion, giving the driver the right to cruise New York City's byways looking for riders, was going for $60,000. That was a lot more than Nash had ever seen at one time in one place in his life. So he did the next best thing: He cloned a cab. For a few hundred dollars, he bought a beat-up 1978 Ford LTD that had once been a cab but had been retired after several hundred thousand miles of bouncing over the city's streets. It was, though, still painted taxicab yellow and could pass any-where for the real thing. Nash set about making it even more real. He carefully painted the going rates on the side, where they should be. He went out and one dark night spotted a parked and unmanned cab. He pilfered the meter and the rate card and made impressions of the license plates and medallion. Then he went home, took some metal and plastic, and turned out replicas of the plates and medallion, affixed them to his cab, installed the meter and rate card, forged a hack license and installed it, and then went off to see what he could make.

His little foray lasted perhaps a week, perhaps a little more, during which he netted himself as much as $250 or $300 a day. Then it all came to a sudden and decisive climax. In one of those almost unbelievable Dickensian coincidences, Avila Narciso was cruising through midtown Manhattan in his cab early one afternoon when he noticed another cab parked at the curb near Forty-fifth Street on Sixth Avenue. He took another look and slammed on the brakes. The parked cab bore exactly the same license plates as the cab he was driving. It couldn't be; it was impossible. Narciso went looking for a cop, found one, and returned. The cab still was there, and the driver, who happened to be Donald Nash, was sitting behind the wheel. The cop asked a few questions, and it didn't take long to realize that Nash was driving a clone, that the medallion and license plates were phonies, as was the hack license inside, and that the meter and rate card were stolen property that happened to belong to Narciso.

Nash was taken in, charged and booked, released on his own recognizance, and given a date to appear in court to answer the charges. Had he had a good lawyer, the chances are that he would have gotten off with a fine and a warning. He had Oestericher as his lawyer. Oestericher advised him to plead guilty, since he'd been caught with the goods. He pleaded guilty. And he was given a twenty-day sentence at the Manhattan Correctional Center.

But the law, of course, moves slowly, and it always is possible to drag things out and delay and delay, and Nash managed to do just that. It wasn't that he wasn't willing to take his medicine, he pled, but the holidays were coming, he had to make all sorts of arrangements to take care of his wife and daughter, his daughter was expecting a baby and he was responsible for that, and a dozen other excuses to delay even more. All his pleas were listened to and, since his offense was not considered an especially heinous one, granted. He was finally given a date to surrender to begin serving his term. That date was Tuesday, April 13, 1982.

Thus, when Torres told him of Oestericher's friend's need, Nash still had time, and he had an increasingly desperate need for money to take care of his family. Yes, he told Torres, he could take care of the job personally, he would do it himself.

Torres called Oestericher and gave him the news. It didn't go down well. Oestericher, knowing Nash, thought Nash was hardly the right person to fulfill Irwin Margolies's order. But Nash had been approached and Nash had agreed, and so be it.

Oestericher went to Margolies and told him. By now, Margolies had begun to have some new thoughts. A beating wasn't good enough for Margaret Barbera. "Wouldn't it be wonderful," he told Oestericher, "if there were no witnesses against me?" And so, he said, Barbera had to go. And not just Barbera. Her very dear friend Jenny Soo Chin had to go, too, because Jenny Soo Chin had worked with and for Barbera at Candor, Jenny Soo Chin knew plenty, and if not as much as Barbera, still enough. And, he had heard, he said, that the government was putting pressure on her as well as on Barbera, and Chin was likely to break.

Set up a meeting with this man, Donald Nash, Margolies ordered. Oestericher called Torres. The meeting was set. A little after noon on a cold, raw day in mid-December, Margolies left Oestericher's, and his, office and made a trip across town, to Ike and Mike's Delicatessen diagonally across West Forty-fifth Street from Vinnie Russo's. Margolies went into the back room and sat down. Across the street, Torres and Nash were watching and waiting. When they saw Margolies arrive, they left their building, crossed the street, entered Ike and Mike's, and went to the back room. Torres introduced Nash to Margolies. They did not shake hands. Torres turned and left. Nash sat down. The two men, Margolies and Nash, got right to the point. They talked in whispers and used hand signals and notes, determined that nobody overhear them.

Margolies had thought it out carefully and fully by then, though he explained to Nash only as much as he thought Nash had to know. He had come armed with photographs of Barbera and Chin, a description of Barbera's BMW, and the location of Barbera's apartment in Ridgewood. These he passed on to Nash. Both of them had to go, preferably at the same time. If that proved impossible, then Barbera was the important one and she should go first. That might just possibly obviate the necessity of taking Chin, might frighten her into complete silence. But that was a long shot. Better to plan to send Chin to the same place, for safety's sake. What was essential, though, was that they be taken when alone, when there were no witnesses, nobody to know what had happened. And when they had been taken, their bodies were to be disposed of so thoroughly that they would never be found, that it would appear to anybody who asked, anybody who investigated that they had just disappeared.

It was Margolies's reasoning that if Barbera and Chin vanished, he would be safe, would be utterly free and clear. Their relationship was no secret; nearly everyone who knew them, in Candor and outside, knew that they were lovers. They made no secret of it, made no effort to conceal it. It was common knowledge, too, that they had made trips together, acting almost as if they were going on a honeymoon, to Europe a couple of times, and elsewhere as well. If suddenly both of them vanished, not a few people would believe that they had finally run off together, to begin a new life someplace where they were not known. Margolies, certainly, intended to say just that to all the right people, all the people who were after him. They had run away, eloped, he would say, and they had taken with them all my diamonds, all my gold, all the money they had stolen, without my knowing it, from Maguire. It would finance them for the rest of their new lives together. If you want to find the diamonds, the gold, the cash, go find them, probably in Europe, where Barbera must have opened up secret numbered bank accounts during her trips there, planning all the time to do this. Who would there be to say nay? He would be off the hook.

Naturally, Margolies told none of this to Nash, offered no explanations. And Nash neither asked nor wanted any. It was enough that Margolies wanted them both killed and had come to him to do the job. He had only one real question: How much? Margolies offered $8,000 for the two. Nash accepted.

16

Nash did not think the Margolies offer a low one, did not consider himself either ill used or ill paid by his procurer. Despite the rumors, the unfounded stories, the movies, murder is not a particularly high-paying job on the scale of contract crimes, and especially not when the would-be hired killer is from outside the ranks of known assassins and has no reputation to back him up. Unlike assaults, robberies, burglaries, and other assorted crimes, there is, with murder, no victim around later to possibly identify the perpetrator. So Nash thought $8,000 for the work neither demeaning nor a small amount, considering that if the killings went according to plan, they could never be traced back to him and there would be nothing to link him to his victims.

As soon as he left that meeting with Margolies at Ike and Mike's, he set about to prepare himself. It is not difficult to get a .22-caliber automatic, and Nash got one someplace, or, perhaps, he already had one, no one is certain. It is just as easy to buy ammunition for a .22, and he got that, too. And it is almost as easy to buy a silencer. Nash picked up a copy of *The Shotgun News* and went through it carefully, marking a few items. Then he turned to his nephew Thomas Dane for help. Dane, for some reason, possessed a license from the Alcohol, Tobacco, and Firearms Bureau to buy and transport weapons in interstate commerce. Dane, then, was the obvious person to do the ordering. Using Dane's license and Dane's address, Nash ordered, to be shipped collect, the eleven component parts that, once assembled, became a silencer, from the Military Accessories Corporation in Cleveland, S.C., for $160, and the sleeve to fit around the parts and attach to the pistol, from Catawba Enterprises in Marietta, Ga. Within days, the packages arrived via United Parcel. Dane paid the bills and turned the packages over to his uncle. Later, Dane would deny ever opening the packages, ever seeing the silencer or even the .22. "I may have asked what was in the packages, I'm not sure," he would say.

Now Nash was ready. He drove out to Ridgewood, parked near Barbera's building, and examined the area, marking the potential places where he might take Barbera and Chin, together or separately, undetected. He waited. The opportunity did not come quickly. But he had the photographs of Barbera and Chin and so could recognize them when they appeared. When Barbera emerged from her building, either alone or with Chin, he followed wherever she went, day after day, noting her schedule, her routine, the places she went, the times she went out alone, and the times when Chin was with her. He kept watching for an opportunity to take them together. It did not come. Perhaps out of some half-realized sense of impending danger, perhaps merely following the normal habits of the years, Barbera rarely was in an isolated place, seemed always to move about in daytime, among other people, on the road with other cars, invariably returning home by dark and not venturing out again. Even when Chin was with her in Ridgewood or she was with Chin in Teaneck, they stayed after dark within the protection of the home.

Nash watched and waited patiently, learning all there was

to learn about the way Barbera lived. And, good family man that he was, he checked in nearly every day to see how his wife, his pregnant stepdaughter, and his nephew were, calling his home and Dane's from pay phones within a radius of a few blocks of Barbera's apartment, always charging those calls to his own home phone.

And he checked in with Margolies, explaining what he was doing, explaining the reasons for the delays. Most of those calls he made from his home or Dane's, calling Oestericher at the lawyer's private unlisted office number, having Oestericher pass on his messages, or reaching Margolies direct at the Oestericher number when Oestericher was away, which happened constantly during December, January, and February, a time when Oestericher was hospitalized off and on with a heart ailment.

Only once during the holiday season did Nash sense an opportunity to fulfill his contract. Barbera and Chin had gone out on a shopping expedition in her BMW one afternoon. They were cruising along one of the main boulevards in Queens, Nash following at a careful distance, close enough always to keep them in sight, not so close as to give them any concern. Suddenly, steam began to pour out from under the hood of the BMW. Barbera pulled over to the side of the road, stopped, got out of the car, and looked at the steaming engine uncertainly. She seemed helpless.

Nash pulled to a stop close behind. He got out of his car and walked toward her and Chin, who also had come out of the car and was standing with Barbera. He later told Oestericher that he considered doing the job then. But it was daylight and there were too many people around. Instead, he decided to play Good Samaritan. He asked if something was wrong, if there was anything he could do to help. Barbera pointed to the overheated engine, to the steam.

Nash went to the front of the car, opened the hood, and took a look. "You've got a broken fan belt," he told her. "Wait a minute. I'll fix it for you." He went back to his own car, the onetime cab, dug around among the junk that filled it, and found a spare fan belt that might suffice for a while, at least.

He returned to Barbera's car, removed the broken belt, replaced it with his spare, and made a few adjustments. "That'll hold for a while," he said. "But you'd better stop at the next gas station to get the right kind."

She thanked him, got back into her car with Chin, and they drove off. Nash waited a moment and then followed.

Only once more would he be so close to Barbera, and only on one other occasion would he be so close to Chin.

Margolies was pressing. Margolies wanted action. Margolies had paid Nash a few thousand dollars down and wanted results. And he had seen none. Through Oestericher and in his own conversations, he demanded to know what was being done, what the reasons were for the delays. Nash tried to placate him. There had been no opportunities to get the two of them alone, without witnesses. There hadn't even been an opportunity to get one of them alone in the right place. For some reason they seemed very careful, they never went out into deserted streets, day or night.

Margolies was very upset. He was sure that soon after the new year, the government would increase its pressures on Barbera and Chin, and he was afraid that one or both of them might capitulate, especially if the government offered a reasonable deal. (It never occurred to him that another former employee, Gaye Broffman, might have something to say to the government and might be saying it.) He told Nash he wanted results, and he wanted them fast. Nash promised results as soon as the holidays were over.

Nash was as good as his word. On January 4, he was back in Ridgewood, resuming his surveillance. He had followed Chin in her red Pontiac station wagon from Teaneck, though now he was driving not his beat-up onetime cab but a silver Chevrolet van he had borrowed from a nephew, Robert Dane, brother of Thomas. He watched Chin enter the apartment building. He waited. Chin did not reappear. After some hours, it was obvious that she was spending the night, a not uncommon practice he had come to understand. He drove home.

Late the next afternoon, January 5, he was back in Ridgewood, once more in the silver van. He had with him, as he

134

always did now, the .22 automatic, silencer attached, fully loaded. He waited. At about seven o'clock, Chin came out of the building and started down the street. She was alone. It was dark. So it would not be the two of them at the same time. It would not even be Barbera first, which was the way Margolies wanted it. It would have to be that the first one to go would be Chin. Margolies wanted results. Nash would give him results. They might not be what he most wanted, but they would have to suffice. He would take Chin now.

He put a ski mask over his head, just in case anyone happened to be around and might see him. He put the loaded gun with the silencer in his pocket. He got out of the van and started down the street after Chin. She turned the corner. He was only a little way behind. He turned the corner. She reached the Pontiac and bent to unlock the door. He came up behind her, thrust her into the car, leaped in after her, and slammed the door. She screamed. It was the last thing she would ever do. He pulled out the silenced automatic and shot her in the head. Then he started the car and drove away, heading for Manhattan.

Once across the Fifty-ninth Street Bridge, he headed west, across Manhattan, until he reached a deserted block far west on Thirty-fifth Street. There he parked. The silver van had followed him in, through Queens, across Manhattan, and to this spot. Who was driving it? The police can only speculate; they are sure they know, but no one has ever been charged as an accessory before and after the fact. In the darkness, in the night, Chin's body was removed from the Pontiac and thrown into the rear of the van. The Pontiac was abandoned. Inside, there were bloodstains and there was a shell casing from a .22 automatic. The van drove off, drove through the tunnel and into New Jersey. And Chin's body vanished forever. Where it was put, Nash has never said, as he has never said anything publicly. But later, when Oestericher asked, he told the lawyer, "Don't worry. It's someplace nobody will ever find it."

But before he performed his magician's trick and made Chin disappear, Nash did one more thing: He took a camera and snapped a picture of the dead woman.

On January 6, the following day, Nash appeared at Oestericher's office. The lawyer was there, and so was Margolies. Oestericher walked out of the office, leaving Nash and Margolies alone. He said later that he didn't want to know what they were going to talk about. He knew enough already.

Nash and Margolies were alone for some time. Then Nash left, and Oestericher returned to the office. Margolies was very angry. According to Oestericher, he said, "That son-of-a-bitch. He killed Jenny. I told him I didn't want her to be the first one. But he said the opportunity was there, and so he did her. And then he showed me a photograph to prove that he'd done it." Margolies pointed to an ashtray. The photograph was there. Margolies had burned it, so Oestericher never saw it whole. But he believed what Margolies said, that it was a photograph of · the bloody, dead body of Jenny Soo Chin.

Nash did one more thing that day. He must have been worried about the van, about the possibilities that there were bloodstains from Jenny Soo Chin in it, that there might be other evidence as well, and that if someone somehow came across it in his possession or in the possession of his nephews, all would not be well. The van had to be ditched. The van was driven across the river into the city and up to the Bronx, and then abandoned on a lonely road near a cemetery. The expectation, of course, was that what would happen to it was what happens to nearly every abandoned car in New York after a few days. Vandals would come along, notice that the van had been parked there and unclaimed for days, and so begin the job of stripping it. Within a week or so, there would be nothing left but a rusting, rotting, empty shell.

The following day, Robert Dane showed up at the Palisades Park, N.J., police department. He wanted to report that his Chevy van had been stolen from a parking place in the town sometime after he had left it on the afternoon of January 5 (the day, of course, when Jenny Soo Chin was abducted and murdered). Inside, he said, was a large quantity of air-conditioning ducts, filters, tools, and other equipment from his small construction business. He intended, he said, to file for

136

recovery of the loss with his insurance company, which he did. (Later Dane would admit that the whole thing had been a hoax. The van, he claimed, had been abandoned in the Bronx in the hopes that it would be stripped and never found, except eventually to be hauled away and thrown on a scrap heap, so he could collect large sums in insurance. He needed the money, and the van was a drain. That was his only reason for doing this, he said.)

Dane and Nash had a right to think that they would get away with this ploy. The chances of an abandoned car being found in the city and returned to the owner are minuscule. But, once more, the near-impossibility became the reality. The vandals passed by and, except for an occasional smack with a stick or a pipe, which left some dents and scrapes, they left the van alone. And after a few weeks, the cops came along, tagged it, called a towing company, and the van was hauled away. A check with the hot car reports revealed that it had been reported stolen. The Palisades Park police were notified; Dane was notified and came to reclaim the van. He complained a little about its condition and complained that the New Jersey license plates that had been on it were there no longer. Somebody must have stolen them, at least. (Nobody did, of course. Dane had simply removed them and, later, turned them over to his uncle.)

With the recovery of the van, the bulletin went out over the FBI line that it should be removed from the hot car list, though the license plates should remain, since they had not been recovered. The order was followed around the country, except in New Jersey, where, for some reason, the van continued to appear as a stolen vehicle.

And then Robert Dane got rid of the van altogether. Once it had been recovered, he turned around and, for a few hundred dollars, sold it to his uncle, Donald Nash. So Nash no longer had to borrow it to use for his purposes. It belonged to him now.

17

Margaret Barbera was a very frightened lady. Her best friend and lover had vanished, and then her car had been found, bloodstains and a cartridge casing inside, so there was a distinct possibility that she was dead. If Barbera didn't know for certain who had done it, or had been behind it, she thought she had a pretty good idea. And then there had been a terrifying phone call to her home, one she wouldn't talk about to anyone. (Telephone records revealed that a phone Donald Nash had access to and often used was the number from which that call had been placed.)

For years she had not had very much to do with her family. But she did not know where else to turn. She called her brother, Barney Barbera, at his home in Pennsylvania, told the jeweler, for that's what he was, that she had to get out of the city, that somebody was after her and she had to get away. She went to him for a visit, stayed a couple of weeks, returned to Ridgewood in February to resume her hunt for Chin, went back to Penn-

138

sylvania again, and, early in March, returned to the city for good, despite what her brother said were his constant pleas to her to leave New York forever, that there was nothing for her there except whatever it was she was afraid of.

She had one other source of help outside her family. She turned to her lawyer, James R. Cooley. She had gone through several other lawyers since the mess began, had left them for one reason or another, had finally found Cooley, who seemed to be what she was looking for. The increasing pressure of the government on her to persuade her to talk and to turn over to the authorities whatever evidence she might have, had begun to get to her. With the disappearance of Chin, she was just about ready to be cooperative, if Cooley could work out some sort of deal for her. She might want to turn Margolies in and see him suffer, but not if doing so meant she would have to go to jail herself. Cooley began the long and difficult negotiations to see what the government would be willing to give in exchange for what she had to give.

Those discussions became more critical and intense once Chin had vanished. For Barbera, terrified now, the important thing was protection against whoever might be after her. According to Cooley, within a few weeks after Chin's disappearance and the discovery of her bloodstained, abandoned car, he and Barbera went to see Stephen Schlessinger, an assistant U.S. attorney who was handling the legal ramifications of the Candor Diamond fraud. They told Schlessinger that Barbera was in fear for her life and that the person she was afraid of was Irwin Margolies.

But at that moment Barbera still was not a cooperative witness, the negotiations not yet at a decisive stage. The government is traditionally not particularly concerned about providing protection for its antagonists, or even those who may be wavering. Perhaps a little fear might push them over, might tip the balance. Further, Schlessinger, like almost everybody investigating the fraud, people who did not know Irwin Margolies well or personally and so had no understanding of what he might be capable, believed that Barbera was the victim of an

139

overactive imagination, was starting from phantoms. Schlessinger responded to the request, Cooley says, by telling them, "Mr. Margolies is not the type of fellow to commit violence, and this is not the type of case where violence is involved." (The government later was to dispute Cooley's charges. John S. Martin, then the U.S. attorney for the Southern District of New York, said, "If they were seriously concerned, they would have put it in writing and would have raised the matter with someone in a supervisory position in the office. To my knowledge, none of that was done.")

The Schlessinger comment was a belief held by just about everybody except Barbera. This was, after all, a white-collar crime, an ingenious fraud to make away with millions. As far as anyone knew at that moment, nobody had been hurt, only money was involved. This wasn't a robbery or a mugging or some other kind of violent crime committed by lowlifes. This was on a more sophisticated level. People on that level just don't resort to violence to keep their fruits. Nobody was likely to go to prison for a long time on this one. If Margolies gave in and returned the diamonds and a good part of the money—not even all of it, just part of it, as was usually the case in this kind of episode—neither the government nor Maguire was likely to come down very hard on him. If he were cooperative, it was just possible that he might get off with a fine and a suspended sentence. At the most, he probably would get a couple of years in one of the prison resorts the government runs for high-class felons.

So despite three or four additional entreaties from Cooley and Barbera for protection in the next weeks and months, the government had no occasion to change its view, at least not until Barbera was in its pocket. No protection was provided. No one, really, thought she needed it.

But Cooley was beginning to make progress in his attempt to negotiate a deal for Barbera. By March, after weeks of long and hard arguments, a bargain was struck. The government would make no promises. It never does. But the indications were that Barbera could expect very lenient treatment, perhaps a suspended sentence, at most a very short spell in a comfortable place in exchange for what she might reveal.

On March 18, 1982, Barbera met with the government attorneys and FBI agents and began to pour out her tale. She told in detail how the fraud had commenced and progressed, who was involved, and who did what when. While she implicated herself, she tried to minimize her role. What she did, she said, was fictionalize books and records and now and then make a suggestion. She did not have access to the bank accounts. Only Irwin and Madeleine Margolies did. She could not write the checks. Only Irwin and Madeleine Margolies could. They were the ones who had done it. With just a little help from her. What she did not tell the prosecutors and did not reveal to Cooley or anyone else was that she had the books that could prove what she was relating, though they might implicate her more than she wanted. She felt they were still her protection, and she was determined to hang on to them for as long as possible.

On March 25, she appeared in court to make her plea. The government had decided to accept a guilty plea to a single count of mail fraud, a felony. In its sentencing memorandum to the judge, it would describe how cooperative she had become, and between the lines anyone could read that the prosecutors were in favor of the greatest leniency. That court session was held *in camera,* in the strictest privacy and secrecy. The government did not want the word to get back to Margolies that Barbera had turned. Now it wanted her safe, even though nobody yet believed that she was in any particular danger. But her testimony was vital to the case that was being built against the diamond manufacturer, and it would be best if nobody knew about it.

Once her plea had been accepted, Barbera was informed that this was just the first step. She would be called in late April to testify before a grand jury, empaneled to hear the evidence in the Candor swindle. When indictments were handed down against Margolies and his wife and others, she could expect to be the government's star witness at their trials.

Somehow, Margolies learned that she was talking. He was furious. Her testimony would put an end to all his dreams, all

141

he had worked for so long and so hard. But if she did not appear before the grand jury, there still might be hope. He got in touch with Nash and railed about the delays. There had already been considerable trouble because Nash had taken so much time, more than three months since Margolies had given him the contract. He had not done what he was being paid to do. Margolies demanded action, without delay.

Nash tried to explain the difficulties. Barbera had disappeared for weeks at a time since he had taken Chin, and whenever she reappeared, she was very careful and watchful. There had been no chance to get at her. Margolies didn't want to hear excuses. He was beginning to believe that Oestericher's initial reaction had been right, that Nash simply was the wrong person for the job, that he should have found somebody else, a true professional. It was too late now to do anything about that. All he could do was prod Nash, make him perform. And Nash was determined to do Margolies's bidding. He did not have much more time in which to do it. On April 13, he had to report to the Manhattan Correctional Center to begin serving his sentence for cloning a cab.

He and his nephew Thomas Dane took a drive up the Hudson into Rockland County, to the Nanuet shopping mall. They stopped at a sporting-goods store. Nash asked to see a .22-caliber rifle and some ammunition. He bought a hundred rounds of ammunition, said he'd think about the rifle, and then left. He went down the road to another sporting-goods store, bought more ammunition, then returned to the first store and this time bought the rifle. That return made the clerk, John Gaine, remember him. Something else made Gaine remember him. As Nash pulled back his jacket to reach for his wallet, Gaine saw the butt of a .22-caliber pistol on his hip. And Gaine remembered that as Nash paid for the rifle, he had laughed and said he wanted it "for a little varmint hunting and target practice."

Target practice, indeed. At home, Nash spent hours practicing with the pistol against the side of his garage, against targets pinned to trees, perfecting his aim.

And he began to track Barbera more intensely. He was out in Ridgewood, around her apartment almost every day now. As usual, he made those collect calls home and to his nephew from the phone booths in the area. But what Nash did not know was that he had been spotted. Not that anybody paid any attention to it then, but he had been spotted, nevertheless. The FBI had agents in the area, doing surveillance on a reputed organized-crime hangout. One of the things the agents do during such an operation is move through the neighborhood, noting the license plates on the cars parked there. On the night of March 31, as the agents roamed the blocks, one of them jotted down the plate numbers of a silver Chevrolet van. Back at headquarters the next day, those numbers were fed into an FBI computer and stored, available for retrieval if anything ever arose linking that van to the organized-crime stakeout or to anything else.

At the beginning of April, suddenly the break that Nash and Margolies had been waiting for came. Nash had been sitting on Barbera through long hours, day and night, away from home more than he wanted to be, for his stepdaughter was about to have her baby. His breaks now were often to call home to see how she was, and then she went into the hospital, and he called there to check on her condition. Then, one morning at the beginning of April, Barbera broke the pattern that Nash had become so accustomed to. She left home early, drove into Manhattan, to West Fifty-fourth Street, stopping in front of the Camera Service Center. She had a job. She had regular hours. She would be out in the open.

Nash watched to make sure. Perhaps somebody at the camera shop mentioned it to her, perhaps she just saw the sign that overhung the roadway, nobody later could be sure, but Barbera needed a place to park her car, and there it was, only a couple of blocks away, Pier Ninety-two, and it was cheap, only $40 a month. On Thursday, April 1, she drove onto the lot, filled out an application, and paid for a month in advance.

Nash continued to tail her, planning his next move. This could have been a diversion, could have been nothing. He followed her in from Ridgewood to Pier Ninety-two on Friday, and again on Monday, April 5. A new pattern in her life had evolved, she was on a regular schedule. And now he had only a week to do what Margolies had paid him to do; on the morning of April 13, he had to report to the authorities and then spend the next few weeks in the slammer. If Margolies was getting desperate, so was he. He moved. That Monday morning, he followed her as she drove up onto the pier. He was stopped at the gate, was told he could not enter, could not park unless he was a monthly customer, was told to drive on through and exit out the next ramp. He did what he was told. But the attendant, obeying the Kinney dictates, made a note of his license plate: New Jersey 192-SFV. Nash, it seemed, had a habit of switching license plates from one of his cars to another, as whim or reason dictated. This one, it turned out later, should have been on a Ford Pinto he owned, not on the van he was driving.

On Tuesday, April 6, Nash took the next step. Barbera drove in from Ridgewood, up onto the pier, parked, and walked over to work at the camera shop. A half hour later, Nash arrived in his van and announced to the attendant, Tom Phillips, that he wanted to rent a monthly space. Phillips handed him an application. Nash filled it out. He wrote his name: Donald Nash. He wrote an address: Rubin Construction, 436 West 45th Street, New York City, and, indeed, Rubin Construction was what he was calling his struggling business. He wrote a telephone number, prefixed by the Manhattan area code so that it appeared to be the construction company's local number; it wasn't. It didn't exist. But if it had been prefixed by the New Jersey area code, it would have been his own home phone. He wrote a license plate number for the Chevrolet van: New York 53924-GH, which was the number that happened to be on the van at that moment, and was the number that belonged on the van, registered to Donald Nash of 436 West 45th Street. But then Nash apparently got a little worried. If it came, identification would be too easy. He crossed out the real plate number and wrote another, 939-HG New York, a plate that had never been issued by the New York Motor Vehicle Department, it later turned out. He handed the completed application to Phillips along with the $40 monthly parking fee in advance and then drove on through and out onto the pier parking lot. The application was put in the Kinney files, along with those of the hundreds of other cars that parked on the pier or had, in the past, parked there.

If Nash intended to take Barbera that day, the weather was against him. It started to snow, and the snow turned into a blizzard, and offices closed early. Nash had all he could do just to drive home to Keansburg. And on Wednesday, the city was digging out and few cars could enter or leave, and offices remained closed. Another day lost, and time was growing short.

On Thursday, April 8, Barbera drove in early in the morning, as was becoming her habit. Nash arrived just before four in the afternoon. He waited. Barbera appeared at about six. But so did others. There were just too many people around for Nash to make his move and get away in safety. Barbera departed. Nash sat in his van on the pier for another fifteen minutes and then drove off.

On Good Friday, April 9, Barbera was on the pier again just after eight. Nash arrived at about three. But Barbera was already gone. The camera shop had let its employees off early because of the holiday. Barbera had another Easter to live.

Monday, April 12. Nash was out of time. It was this day or never. He would begin serving his time the next morning, and by the time he got out, it would be too late for Margolies, for Barbera would have talked before the grand jury by then. Nash had spoken with Margolies once more over the weekend, had heard the rage in his employer's voice, had promised that it would be done on Monday. And the more he thought about it, the more Monday seemed the ideal time. He would do it, get away, get rid of the body, and then, in the morning, report and go to jail. Let people look for him if somehow they stumbled on something, though if all worked as he and Margolies had planned and hoped, nobody would. Barbera would simply have disappeared, and there were few who would miss her immediately. By the time somebody did, no one would be sure just when she had gone. And if nobody looked for her right away, it would not be until the end of the month, when her parking permit expired and her car still was there, that anybody would realize that she was nowhere around. Margolies then would be able to tell the story he had concocted: Barbera had sent Jenny Soo Chin ahead and now she had joined her somewhere, probably in Europe, with all Candor's diamonds and all Candor's cash. And Nash? He would have been in jail. What better place to hide?

At about five in the afternoon, he drove up on the pier.

At about six, Barbera appeared.

146

PART
FOUR
CHASE

18

Tuesday, April 13. The chase was on. There was just one trouble: At this stage, nobody knew whom he was chasing. But the mayor was incensed. This was the kind of thing that just didn't happen in his city, and he wanted action fast. The police commissioner was promising action—publicly, at least—but he knew the kind of action he was going to get right away might well be action for action's sake. The public was outraged. This hadn't been mobsters killing mobsters, something people could basically ignore, could dismiss with a sense that maybe the guys who got it deserved it and the guys who gave it would one day get the same thing in their turn and, besides, good riddance to bad rubbish. This had been the murder, cold-blooded, of three innocent bystanders who had merely tried to come to the aid of a woman in trouble, and their reward had been a bullet in the head. It gave pause; it gave a feeling that nobody really was safe in this city. The press, especially the sensational press, was at its most sensational, sensationalizing what already was sen-

149

sational enough. There were a thousand rumors, and most of them appeared in the papers. There had been not one but two or more killers. There had been accomplices overseeing the job and reporting its success, via car telephone, to an unknown employer and referring to the killer as "the fall guy." It had been a mob hit done by a professional; one detective in the organized-crime task force was quoted as theorizing that the killer was from one of the syndicate families and "he'll probably be dead by the end of the week; mob hits are supposed to be done anonymously; they don't like fanfare." Almost everybody any reporter talked to had an opinion, and those opinions were diverse, and those opinions were printed.

Nobody but a minor bureaucrat in the criminal-justice system noticed that Donald Nash didn't keep his appointment that morning. He failed to surrender to the authorities to begin serving his term for cloning the cab. That bureaucrat did what he was supposed to do: He went to court and had a judge swear out a bench warrant for Nash's arrest. It was all part of the system, the way things are done and, in the normal course, it would have meant very little. Nash's offense had been so trivial that to expect the cops to go out and look for him on that warrant would have been expecting too much from an already undermanned and overworked department. So nobody then except that bureaucrat thought much about the fact that Nash didn't show when he was supposed to; it happened all the time, and even the bureaucrat probably forgot all about it once he had done his duty and gotten the warrant and filed it.

At Midtown North, the hard and convoluted task of trying to make sense of the pieces that were in hand and trying to find all the missing pieces had begun. Almost the first thing done that morning was to set up a task force to handle the investigation. In the chain of command, Captain Eugene Burke was in charge and Lieutenant Dick Gallagher was assigned to run the operation. But it was, in reality, the case of the men who would go out and run down the leads. There was, of course, Richie Chartrand, and he was joined by Bobby Patterson. John Wales, a cop since 1961, a detective since 1971, much of that time in Midtown North, a large man in size and girth, garrulous, with a thousand stories and anecdotes to illustrate every eventuality and situation, had been off the day of the murders. When he arrived on the thirteenth, he went onto the task force. So, too, did Detective Richie Bohan, another large man and another longtime veteran, and Augie Sanchez, a small, tough cop whose manner was enough to frighten the unwary and those who had something to hide. And Sergeant Tom Kenney was detached from his usual duties for work on the task force. Do a good job, solve this thing and bring in the guy, they were promised, and you'll all get rewards, promotions to the next grade for detectives, pay at the next rank on the official ladder, and more.

By midmorning the FBI showed up, Special Agents Don Richards, Bob Paquette, John Truslow, and others. They offered themselves and all the facilities of the Federal Bureau of Investigation, anything they and the agency could do to help. They would be, they explained, a support service in what was about to become a joint investigation of the murders of three innocent bystanders and one, or possibly two, witnesses in a federal investigation. "That is a very fancy way of saying, if you need something, you ask us and we will do it," says Chartrand. "And this was one of the very few times that I know that the New York City Police Department and the FBI really worked in a very cohesive manner. There was a free-flowing input of information. We all had to introduce ourselves to each other that morning, and we all had to satisfy ourselves that we would trust each other, and we had to establish who was going to handle what. The ground rules were set up. Everything would be handled out of Midtown North, and from that early stage, the federal agents worked out of our office. They would show up at our office on time. They were always ready and willing to assist."

Assist they did, and without delay. Physically, the FBI wanted its agents, and so, by association, the New York cops, to be comfortable, to have all the best and the most modern, and the FBI has plenty of money to provide. "It was unbelievable," John Wales remembers. "I never saw anything like it. We got tables, typewriters, telephones, everything. We had telephones with no numbers. The expenses were astronomical and we didn't even

151

get a bill on it. Nothing. And the telephone bill for the first month, I was told, was more than six hundred dollars. Now, the police department, it doesn't go six hundred dollars in six months for the phone, and then it screams. But we got everything instantly. All we had to say is, 'We need it.' I mean, they pushed buttons and things worked. Like banks. They got us all the records, accounts, everything. Stuff you never could get. You get on a regular homicide, it's impossible, it's on microfilm, they tell you, and we don't know where it is. But this time they pushed the button and we went right down and they had it right waiting for us. But now, anything we wanted, we got. We got a subpoena and it was honored, by the banks and by everybody. I mean, normally I get a subpoena and give it to them and, somehow, they've lost everything. Banks especially. They never really give you anything. But here, anything we requested, we got, with a minimum of trouble."

Action was what was being demanded, and in those first days, there was plenty of action, running off in every direction. "The only thing we knew for sure," Wales says, "was that a man who shot some people got into a van and drove away. We had no good identification of the man. And the van, basically, it was white or light-colored with stripes on the side and it had a sliding door on the side. That's it. No year, no make, no license plate at all."

Maybe, somebody said, some of those people on the *Rotterdam* were taking pictures when the liner was leaving the pier, and maybe they got a shot of the killer waiting in the parking lot. So the word went out. Contact the ship and ask the people who had been taking pictures to turn in the rolls so the cops could go through them. It was a long shot, but at least it was a shot, it was something. (The rolls were turned in, developed, examined, and revealed nothing.)

Maybe, somebody suggested, somebody was looking out of a window in one of the buildings overlooking the pier parking lot, and maybe that somebody saw something and didn't realize what he was seeing, but under questioning he might remember. So detectives were sent to the nearby buildings and talked to tenants from whose windows the surface of the parking lot could be seen. Nobody had seen anything.

Everybody had an idea. "Did anybody check to see if there was an airplane flying overhead?" Wales remembers. "You might say, what a stupid idea. But if one of the big shots suggested it, you did it. God forbid, somebody writes a letter in and says, 'Dear Police Department, I was going back home on the plane and I was looking out the window and I saw a strange thing. I saw what looked like this man playing tag. It looked like he had something flashing in his hand. I didn't think anything of it until I got home and my cousin told me, gee, you just missed a big shooting in New York. And I said, oh, my God, I saw the whole thing.' If you get that kind of a letter and you didn't go and check the airports, you can imagine. But if it's just me and another guy, you can't waste time going around looking at everything. If you don't have the men, you don't have the time, you can't do that. But if you have so many men, like we did on this thing, you can do it. When you have a million guys, just to keep them going, because they stagnate if they're hanging around, the boss will come in and say, hey, you and you, go and do this, you and you, go and do that. You get things going and everybody keeps going and maybe you come up with something." But it didn't happen with the planes or the buildings or the ship or nearly anything else.

Still, there was the van. They had that. "My function at the beginning," Wales says, "was looking for the van. We figured that if we didn't find it in the first day or two or three, that'd be it and we'd never find it. So there was a citywide alarm out on that van. Every single police car in New York City was ordered to survey their sector—that is, drive around their entire sector and look for any van resembling the description of this van. Anything at all and then they would call our office. They had parking lots and garages, they were to survey them. They were to go inside and see if there was anything that fit this description. Then the calls started coming in. We got a call from Brooklyn. They found a van in the parking lot that fits the thing. We went out there. The van's been there for seven days, hasn't been moved, has a flat tire, a broken windshield. It's not our van. Everybody's calling in. We'd rather they call in than pass it, take it on their own. We got vans that had hinge doors instead of sliding doors. We had one van that was down by the Brooklyn Navy Yard. A Volkswagen. But it was a camper. And it had a bed inside. It had all kinds of shit inside. No way in the world that a man could pull a body in.

"So now we're eliminating vans. Anything that seems good, we go and sit down and completely process the van, take prints, examine for blood or red or any stains. Then there was the problem of sanitation. The crushers, where they tow away abandoned cars. That was done. The helicopters were searching the outlying areas, Kennedy Airport, Canarsie, any swamp, anything like where it could possibly be. Everything was checked. And we came up empty."

The killer himself? It was generally agreed by everybody on the case, the New York City detectives and the FBI agents, that he was a hired gunman. But who had done the hiring? Richards and Paquette had filled in Gallagher, Chartrand, and the others on the details of the Candor swindle, as much as they thought the New York cops needed to know. But for the moment at least, they ruled out Margolies as the man behind the murders. Murder just wasn't something that happened in this kind of a case. It was too extreme, too out-of-the-ordinary. White-collar criminals, swindlers, don't resort to violence. It's not the pattern. But if not Margolies, who? Some of the investigators thought Jenny Soo Chin's husband the most likely suspect, given his wife's disappearance and probable murder, given the relationship between his wife and Barbera, given what they saw as his reaction, or lack of it. Some thought perhaps a spurned boyfriend of Barbera's or someone unknown for some unknown reason.

But for the moment, the man behind the murders, and surely there was one, was less important than the murderer himself, and, despite the rumors, no one had any doubts that there was only one killer. If they could identify and find him, the rest would fall into place.

19

Donald Nash knew he had to run. His only hope was in flight. And he was not sanguine about that. He called Oestericher's private unlisted number. He told Oestericher he was convinced that he was going to get caught. But if Margolies would agree to hire and pay for a lawyer for him and see that his family was taken care of, he would never say a word about who had hired him. Further, he said, he wanted the balance of the $8,000 due him for the murder of Barbera, and he thought he deserved an additional payment for the terrible thing he had to do when those three CBS people walked in on him when he was putting Barbera into the van.

Oestericher listened, said he would contact Margolies and then get back to Nash. He called Margolies, told him what Nash wanted. Margolies said, not a penny more for Barbera. She deserved to be dead because she was not trustworthy and she had proved to be an enemy of his. But, yes, Nash did deserve something extra because of that unexpected snag that had put him in such extreme danger. If Nash were caught and agreed never to talk about the reasons why he had done these dastardly deeds, then Margolies would take care of him: He would find him a lawyer and pay the bill; he would provide for his family; he would pay the balance owed on Barbera; and he would ante up an additional $5,000 for the CBS murders.

Oestericher passed the word on to Nash. Nash accepted the terms. Oestericher reported to Margolies and said the money would have to be paid immediately. Margolies agreed. It was not hard for him to gather that much cash, in $100 bills. He and Madeleine Margolies counted it to make sure it was all there. Then they packaged it. The neatly wrapped bundle was turned over to one of their sons, who bore it to a Federal Express office. When it was ready, Nash sent a messenger to Federal Express to retrieve it and deliver it to him in Keansburg. (Some weeks later, a very worried Madeleine Margolies paid a call on Henry Oestericher. Can the FBI get fingerprints off money? she asked. Why? Oestericher countered. Because, she explained, she had helped count and package the money that had been sent to Nash, and if they could get her fingerprints, she was in a great deal of trouble. Oestericher considered that and then said he did not think bills retained fingerprints.)

Now Nash began to prepare for his flight. He and his nephew Thomas Dane went out shopping. They went to an auto supply store near home, bought black auto paint and a number of sporting decals. It was on to Newark Airport from there. Nash retrieved the silver van. But on his way out, he decided to play a little game and so gain additional protection. Instead of handing in the parking ticket as he departed, he tucked it up under the sun visor on the windshield, told the attendant he had misplaced it, had a little argument about how much he owed and the time he had entered (he claimed it had been early the day before, which, if believed, would have put the van in the parking lot before the murders on the pier), finally settled up for what the attendant demanded, and said he was going to file a claim for the lost ticket and the charges. Then, followed by Dane, he drove back to Keansburg. Over the next several hours, inside his garage, they spray-painted the van black and affixed the decals of eagles, bear, and fish around the sides. When the paint was dry, Nash drove back to Newark Airport, parked the now-black van in the long-term lot, and then returned to Keansburg in Dane's car.

He would have liked to have begun his trip immediately. He could not. The money from Margolies had not yet arrived and he had to wait for it, wait for the word that it was at Federal Express, send his messenger, and know that he really possessed it. That took a few days. By Friday, April 16, the money had been collected. The first thing Nash did was use some of it, some of the $5,000 for the CBS disaster and the balance from the Barbera-Chin contract, to pay off a second mortgage on his home. The rest, something over $2,500 in $100 bills, he kept, stuffing them into his wallet, to see him through the hard days to come.

On Saturday, April 17, he was ready to move. At about midmorning, Dane arrived and picked him up. They went on another shopping excursion, this time to a string of sporting-goods stores between Keansburg and Newark. He spread some of his new money around, buying sleeping bags, fishing poles, a portable stove, a portable lantern, blankets, a portable AM-FM cassette recorder-radio, a small portable television set, hunting clothes, boxes of food that would not spoil, and a lot more. It was as though he were planning to establish himself as huntsman of the year.

By late in the afternoon, he had bought all he thought he would need for a long stay in the woods, or at least on the road. Dane drove him back to Newark Airport and let him out at the entrance to the long-term parking lot. A few minutes later, the black van, Nash driving, emerged from the lot. He had changed license plates once more; this time the van bore New Jersey plates.

A few miles from the airport, Nash pulled to the side of the road. Dane's car, which had been following, pulled up behind. For the next fifteen or twenty minutes, the two men moved all the camping and hunting equipment, all the newly purchased supplies and more, including the .22-caliber rifle Nash had purchased earlier in Rockland County, from Dane's car to the van. When they were done, Dane returned to his car and drove off. Nash got into the van, turned it onto the New Jersey Turnpike, and headed south.

What he did not know was that ever since he and Dane had left his home in Keansburg, they had been followed by FBI agents. Less than fifteen minutes before that morning departure, the FBI had arrived outside the house to begin surveillance, had hardly placed themselves before Nash was on the way out. Had they arrived fifteen minutes later, he would have been gone and, in all likelihood, might never have been found.

20

After fruitless days of search for any clue to identify the hired killer (and they were certain he had been that), for any sign of the van he had used to transport Barbera's body and then flee, the frustration of the investigators was evident. It was three and a half days since the murders, and they were no closer to finding what they were seeking than they had been at the start.

John Wales had an idea. He went to Gallagher. He was going over to the pier, he said, to the Kinney office. He was going to go through the whole operation, learn as much as he could, and he was going to go through the monthly parking applications. Since they were sure the killer had been after Barbera, he had to have known her habits. If she parked on the pier, maybe he did, too. And if he did, it was not unlikely that he had applied for a monthly space about the same time she did. It was worth checking.

· The more he learned in conversation at Pier Ninety-two, the more Wales thought he was on the right track. Nobody, he

159

was told, was allowed up on the parking pier unless he had a monthly permit, and the plate numbers of every car entering and leaving were noted to make sure there were no freeloaders. The only exceptions, the only times visitors were permitted on the pier, was when a ship was docking or departing. Of course, that Monday there had been a ship sailing. So it was possible the van had been used by one of the visitors. But if he had been tracking Barbera, it was unlikely. He was probably a regular.

Wales turned to the applications. "There were about three hundred of them," he says, "but we were looking specifically for vans, so that narrowed it. We found that maybe twenty or thirty vans had taken spaces, monthly spaces, but none of them had done it after the time Barbera put in hers. In fact, between April first and April twelfth, there had been only five applications for monthly spaces, and only one of them had been a van. And that application kind of stood out. First of all, it was a van, and second of all, it had a cross-out on it. I mean, it had one plate number and that was crossed out and another one written in. So I took that application down to the kid at the gate and asked him what he knew about it. He said, yeah, I remember a guy with a silver van. He came through one day and he wrote down the wrong plate number and I made him write down the correct one."

That was the start. Wales was getting very interested. He asked to look at the time sheets, when the van entered and left and when Barbera's BMW entered and left. The tickets were incomplete, but they were complete enough to show a pattern, to show that the silver van could very well have timed its arrivals and departures to coincide with Barbera's presence on the pier.

Wales was sure he had it now. But he wanted to make certain. He headed back for the office with the application, called down to the Department of Motor Vehicles to authenticate the plate. Back came the identification: it belonged to a van registered to a Donald Nash of West Forty-fifth Street. Wales called down to see if this Nash had an arrest record. He did, had been convicted and sent to prison once, had been convicted and fined several other times for a variety of offenses, and, perhaps as significant as anything, he was a fugitive; there

160

was a bench warrant out for him for failure to surrender to begin serving a short sentence.

"I knew I had him," Wales said. "So I looked around and I said to Chief Ponzini, 'I got the killer right here.' He thought it was a joke, since I was the kind of guy that tells little jokes every day, every single day, and he never believes me. I said, 'No, I mean it. If I don't have the killer, if this isn't the killer, I'll buy everybody lunch,' and there were about forty people in the office right then. And I said, 'If it is the killer, I want to get second-grade detective out of this.' He says. 'Okay, if you've got the right guy, you get second-grade.' I never got second-grade." And despite the promises, nobody else ever got anything, either.

Everything finally was falling into place. They had the plate number of the van and they had the name of the owner even if, right then, they had an address in New York for him and not his home in New Jersey. But it was a start, the first real start. The plate number was turned over to the FBI, and the agents ran it through their computer to see if anything turned up. "Bingo!" Wales says. "It comes back as being a block away from Barbera's house. I mean, they had made an observation of the van as being there. They were doing an organized-crime surveillance, an entirely different case that had nothing to do with this, and they went around the block and copied down all the plate numbers, and one of them was his. And this time, they had the address in Jersey."

It was late Friday night, though, before all the pieces had come together, and it was Saturday morning before the FBI moved, headed for Keansburg to begin surveillance on Donald Nash. They arrived as he was leaving.

With Nash on the move, the immediate question was whether to stop him and pick him up right then or let him go, tail him to see where he was heading and if he was going to meet somebody. The decision was to wait and tail, especially since there was uncertainty. The van registered to Nash and the van on the pier had been a silver one. The one Nash was driving was black. It could be a different one, then. The FBI wanted to get close enough at some point, without Nash being alerted and alarmed, to check the vehicle identification number (VIN) on the dashboard to see if it matched the silver van's.

In cars, constantly alternating places so that Nash would suspect nothing, in helicopters and planes, the federal agents kept pace with the van as it moved steadily south. By nightfall, Nash had reached Lancaster, Pa. He pulled off the Pennsylvania Turnpike and stopped at a Holiday Inn. There he spent the night.

In darkness later that night, the FBI moved in on the van. The VIN was unreadable, masked by paint. A scraping of black paint was taken from the van, to be tested to see if it was, as suspected, fresh.

The decision was made to let him continue, and to keep constant watch, to make sure he was never out of sight of his pursuers, to wait for the opportunity to make sure of the VIN before taking him. They now had additional evidence linking Nash to the silver van, if they needed it. That morning, a six-year-old neighbor of Nash had been playing in Waackack Creek, which ran directly behind Nash's home. Floating in the creek, she found some papers. She brought them to her mother, who turned them over to authorities. Those papers included an insurance identification card and insurance policy issued on March 2 to Donald Nash covering a silver van, containing the VIN and the license-plate numbers. Those plate numbers matched the ones the FBI had jotted down that March night in Ridgewood and the numbers Nash had written in on his Kinney parking application. Still, everyone thought it important to let him continue on his way, until the VIN could be made and, perhaps, until he met up with somebody, a somebody who conceivably could be his employer.

Nash drove on through the next day, Sunday, reaching Milton, West Virginia, at dusk. He pulled off the road and into a campground. That night, he slept in the van. The agents could not approach.

Back in New York, the cops and the FBI were getting a little nervous. The tracking had gone on for two days, was about to go into a third. So far, they had been lucky. They had not lost Nash. But what if they did? What if he turned off the road, undetected? What if somehow he managed to slip by? The decision was made to precipitate a little action. A request was made to the Kentucky State Police to set up roadblocks and check the papers and VINs of every car that went through. That way, they could make certain of the identification number of the black van. Supposedly, that was all that was wanted. Then Nash would be permitted to continue to wherever he was going, to his rendezvous, if there was one.

About noon, on Interstate 64 about twenty miles from Lexington, Nash reached the roadblock. He handed over his papers to the state trooper, who examined them, made note of the numbers and other information, handed them back, and waved Nash on. Nash drove away.

As Nash drove on, the trooper radioed the information about the van back to headquarters. There it was put on the computer for a check. Months before, during the aborted attempt by Robert Dane to ditch the van and collect the insurance, he had reported it stolen. When it was recovered, the alarm for a stolen vehicle was supposedly canceled. But because of the missing license plates, the alarm actually remained in force, and now the word came back to the Kentucky troopers that the black van that had just passed through was, according to the VIN, a stolen vehicle. The troopers set out on a chase, and, less than a half hour later, twenty-five miles down the road, they found it. It was parked by the side of the road. Nash was sitting on a campstool, eating fried chicken for lunch, chicken he was cooking on his new camp stove. He was put under arrest. He offered no resistance, surrendered meekly, and was taken to the barracks in Frankfurt.

"I said to Captain Burke," John Wales remembers, "when they told us about the roadblocks that they're going to stop the car and something's going to be wrong and they're going to pop him. I'll bet you, I said. He says, no they won't. Well, they did."

Indeed, they did. But Dick Gallagher adds, "I'll tell you this, it was no accident. They knew exactly what they were doing. They were holding the bag. The FBI was tailing this guy, not the New York City Police Department. And if that son-of-a-bitch ever got away from them, which could have happened, who's going to look like the biggest idiots in the world? Not us. They got nervous and they cut it off. But, what the hell, how long were you going to go on with this stupid thing? I don't blame them. If it had been us, we'd probably have taken him before he got out of Jersey."

So now they had Nash and they had the van, and both were safely ensconced in Kentucky, for the moment at least. But there was the realization that unless they did something fast, they could lose both. It would not take long for the news to travel south that the van was not, after all, a stolen vehicle, that it legally belonged to Nash. When that happened, he would get into it and drive on his way. They moved on two fronts to stop that.

There was the bench warrant out on Nash as a fugitive from justice for failing to surrender on April 13 and begin serving his twenty days for the conviction for cloning a taxicab medallion. Into court went a Manhattan assistant district attorney to obtain approval for a request to Kentucky for Nash's extradition back to New York on that fugitive warrant. Normally, such a request would be taken under advisement; the court would consider the merits. When the charge was minor, as inconsequential as this one, it might normally have resulted only in laughter and sarcasm, not official approval. But this was different. The assistant district attorney made his motion. It was granted on the spot. Down to Kentucky went the request for extradition. And down to Kentucky went Detectives John Wales and Bobby Patterson to bring Nash back, if the Kentucky court agreed to honor the extradition request.

Down to Kentucky, too, went Detective Richie Chartrand and a Manhattan assistant district attorney, and with them went FBI Agent Bob Paquette and a federal lawyer. They wanted a look through the van and what might be in it. "We get down there," Chartrand says, "and we make an application for a search warrant. The judge is a very precise and accurate man. He not only wants to know why we want to search the van, he wants to know where the van is, and it's in a Kentucky State Police garage, and he wants to know how many yards and how many feet from the roadway it is, at what intersection that is. We provide him with that very precise information and he grants us a search warrant. And now we do a search of the vehicle. We do many searches. We spend eleven and a half hours searching the van. We have a team of pathologists from the Kentucky State Police. We have forensic experts. We have a seven-man and one-woman search team. And every time we go into the van, we come back out with more. We do everything according to the book, what was retrieved, who retrieved it, who took possession of what, and we photographed everything before it was removed from the van."

The list of items that was discovered and removed from the van runs to pages and numbers more than 150. It included some very interesting and incriminating things. Though Nash had tried to do a thorough job of cleaning the interior at the same time he was painting the van, there was much he had missed. And so Chartrand, Paquette, and their search teams and experts came up with a set of New York license plates, the same plates that had been on the van when it was registered to park on Pier Ninety-two and that had been spotted by the FBI near Barbera's apartment. They found wooden matches. They found eleven rounds of live .22-caliber ammunition in the back and another live round in the pocket of a light-colored windbreaker. They found splashes of blood on the floor in the rear, on the doors and door handles, on the ceiling, and elsewhere in the van. Nash had tried to scrub them away when he cleaned the van, but enough traces remained for good samples to be collected from every spot where the blood was discerned. In the well underneath the driver's seat, they discovered a spent .22-caliber shell casing. Impressions were taken of the van's tires, and scrapes of paint from the outside. They found a parking ticket from the Newark Airport long-term parking lot under the visor.

"Everything," Chartrand says, "was put into the custody of Paquette and myself, with the exception of the shell casing. I took possession of that." And Gallagher says, "He painted the van, changed the plates, drove all that distance, and the asshole's asshole is approximately ten inches from the missing fourth shell casing all the while. After shooting Barbera, the shell casing apparently ejected into the van. No wonder we went crazy looking for that fourth shell casing." It was only right. The rules of the game were that the murders belonged to the New York cops, and the FBI was helping out only because its major witness in a fraud case had been among the murdered. The casing, of course, might be directly related to the murders.

Chartrand and Paquette made the next plane north, heading back for New York. Chartrand took the shell casing to the police lab for examination; Paquette took the blood samples and other evidence to FBI labs for analyses. What came back was damning. The shell casing found in the well of the van identically matched the shell casing found in Jenny Soo Chin's car and the three shell casings found next to the bodies of the three CBS victims. All five had been fired in the same .22-caliber pistol. The impressions of the tire tracks were a match with the tire tracks found on the pier. Some of the blood samples matched Margaret Barbera's blood; while there were no blood samples available from Jenny Soo Chin, other samples found in the van were consistent with the blood of an Oriental woman.

"You've got one hell of a case against the van," an assistant district attorney told Chartrand when he laid it all out for him. "But that's it. What about Nash?"

Nash was in jail in Kentucky, waiting for a hearing to decide whether the state would honor New York's request for extradition. Wales and Patterson arrived to take him into custody and return him, should the court agree. Nash appeared at the hearing with a local attorney, Larry Cleveland of Frankfurt. The judge read the request, looked at Nash. Did Nash agree to waive extradition and permit himself to be escorted back to New York? Cleveland responded that Nash did, indeed, waive extradition. The judge looked at Cleveland, looked at Nash, and asked where Nash had found his lawyer, since he was a stranger in the city. Nash said he had looked through the telephone book's listing of lawyers and chosen Cleveland. Was there any particular reason? the judge asked. Because, Nash replied, he had once had a good time in Cleveland and so the name might be a good omen. The judge looked at him. He had read the papers, knew the reports, knew that some of the papers were calling the man before him Donald Bowers. So the judge said, "Tell me, did you choose the name Nash because your parents once had a good time in the back seat of a Nash?"

With that, the judge ordered Nash turned over to Wales and Patterson. He summoned the two detectives to his office to wait while he signed the papers. In the office with them was Larry Cleveland, putting in a claim for a few hundred dollars as his fee for representing Nash, a claim against $2,500 in $100 bills found in Nash's wallet when he was picked up. The judge took Cleveland's request under advisement. Until he, or somebody else, knew whether the money Nash had actually belonged to him, he wasn't about to start disbursing it among the claimants. He signed the papers so that Wales and Patterson could take custody of their prisoner. Wales, the eternal jokester, suddenly interjected, "Your Honor, I want to ask you something. About deathbed statements, declarations, that kind of thing."

The judge said, "What?"

Wales said, "Suppose we're riding in the plane. I know you admonished us not to talk to the defendant here, and our district attorney in New York told us the same thing. But suppose we're in the plane and the pilot comes over the loudspeaker and says, 'Ladies and gentlemen, we've developed engine trouble, both engines are going out any second and the plane is going to crash.' And all of a sudden, the plane does a turnover and starts heading down. As it's going down, Nash turns around to me and says, 'Listen, I want to make a clean breast of things before we go out. I really killed all those people.' And at that point, the plane levels out and flies straight. Would that be considered, would that be eligible to take into court? Did I violate his Miranda rights? And what if my brother happens to be the pilot on this plane? It's an amazing coincidence, but what if it was so?"

The judge stared at Wales. "You're kidding," he said. "You're brother's really a pilot on this plane?"

Laughing, Wales remembers the scene. "He thinks," Wales

says, "I'm going to do that. He thinks I can make the plane go into a tailspin. It's a commercial plane, a hundred people on that plane. Then he knew I was kidding. But it was a thing there for a minute."

The two New York detectives took Nash out to the airport and boarded the plane with him. On the plane, too, was an army of New York reporters, flown down to witness the events in Frankfurt. On the first leg of the trip, from Frankfurt to Roanoke, Va., Wales and Patterson kept Nash separated from the reporters. It wasn't hard. Nash had nothing to say to anyone. "Our entire conversation was, 'You want a drink?' 'You want a sandwich?' 'You want to go to the bathroom?' That was it. He just sat there staring out of the window, staring into space," Wales says.

In Roanoke, there was a layover for an hour or so. Back in New York, word had just reached Chartrand from the police lab that the shell casing found in the van was a match with those found on the pier and in Chin's car. Wales heard the news when he called the office from the airport in Virginia. But, he was told, this was strictly secret. The news was going to be held tightly, not let out to anyone.

Back on the plane, Wales and Patterson, knowing what Nash did not know, had a feeling of some elation. And they thought they knew something the reporters didn't know, either, which made them feel even better. "The reporters on the plane," Wales said, "they see us and they come back where we're sitting. They want to talk to Nash. So I said, 'Listen, the guy's a prisoner. We're instructed by the court and we're not going to talk to him. You can't really ask him anything pointed, and I doubt if he's going to answer you, and we don't want you to annoy the guy. But if he wants to talk to you, that's okay with us. We have no objections at all.' So now, one of the reporters says to him, 'How do you feel now that the bullets match? The bullet found in your van matches the bullets found on the pier?' I don't know how they knew about it. They must have got it from somebody down in ballistics. When this guy says this, Nash, there was a visible change in him. His eyes are misty. You could see how upset he was. Now, like he realized. He thought it was all bullshit, that we got him on the misdemeanor thing. Now he realizes that we're doing some more things, things that he doesn't know about, especially with the bullets. It was like he was all of a sudden all screwed up. Let me tell you, we were annoyed with the fucking newsies for doing that. It put us in a bad position. Now we've got a guy we might have a problem with. We don't want him to try to escape or go crazy or go wild. But he never said anything. But you could see an actual visible change in his mood. He looks like he seemed almost ready to cry."

They landed in New York. Nash was hustled to the Brooklyn House of Detention. Theoretically, he was there only to serve his twenty days.

21

They had a very good case against the van. Now they began to build an even better case against Donald Nash. Some of the pieces came through the drudgery of good, solid police work. Some came almost through accident, because somebody knew somebody, because somebody remembered something that hadn't seemed very important at the time.

Everything was done according to the rules. When a search warrant was needed, a search warrant was obtained before anyone went anywhere. When somebody had to be warned of his Miranda rights, he was warned of his rights. Nobody was about to do anything that would jeopardize this case.

With those search warrants in hand, the New York cops, the FBI, and local New Jersey cops descended on Nash's house in Keansburg. Scuba divers went to work in the creek that flowed behind it, laboriously sifting through the mud, screening whatever they brought up. In addition to all the junk that filled the creek bottom, they dredged up a .22-caliber shell casing. It matched the five they already had, and it had been fired from the same pistol. Into and around the garage went the investigators, and immediately several very interesting things attracted their attention. On the floor of the garage was the outline of the van in black paint, the same black paint that had been used to recolor it. And, indeed, Nash's nephew Thomas Dane admitted that he had gone shopping with his uncle for that paint and had helped him with the job. There was nothing suspicious about it, Dane maintained. The van had a number of chips and scrapes and dents, and grease stains that just wouldn't come off, so repainting was the only solution.

In the outside walls of the garage, toward the rear, there were a number of small holes, like the holes made by bullets fired through during target practice. But there were no holes on the inside. However, when the garage was measured, the outside proved to be larger than the inside. The investigators went to the inside rear and found a door leading to a small storage room, now nearly empty. The walls of that room were peppered with bullet holes, and on the floor there were other shell casings, all from the same gun. An intensive search was made for that gun, of course, but it was never found. Not that it was needed. With all those shell casings that had been fired from it and that could now with a certainty be tied to Nash, it would have been nice to have but it was, in reality, extraneous.

Almost at the same time, other cops were checking on that Newark Airport parking ticket that had been found under the visor of the van. With it, they could now prove not only that the van had been in the long-term parking lot on the night of the murders, but that it had entered some time after those killings, long enough after so that Nash could have had plenty of time to do what he was then suspected of doing. They went through every parking ticket from the lot for that period, accounted for every one except that ticket that had been issued to the car that had followed Dane into the lot. Now they had that one, from the visor of Nash's car. It had been issued to a silver van; it was found in a black van.

There was more. "By chance," says Chartrand, "I get a

171

phone call from a guy I used to work with, a retired detective. He says, 'My future son-in-law works in a sporting-goods store in Rockland and he remembers this fellow that you now have arrested, that he came into the sporting-goods store and he purchased ammunition.' He tells us the type of ammunition. We ultimately go back up there and they have a record of the transaction."

It was all closing in around Nash. The FBI computer check showed that his van had been parked near Barbera's house. That van had become a regular parker on the pier within days of Barbera, had entered and left in a pattern that showed it was tracking her. There was the record of phone calls, available because of Nash's ingrained habit of charging calls to his home phone. There was the series of calls from public phones out in Ridgewood, within blocks of Barbera's house. There was the call from his office on Forty-fifth Street to his home in Keansburg, and a second call within a very short time of the murders from the booth across the street from FBI headquarters in lower Manhattan to Dane, and that call had been made only a short distance from the alley where Barbera's body was found.

It was, of course, all circumstantial. The one witness to the murders on the pier, Angelo Sicca, could not identify Nash, and the two teenage witnesses to the abduction of Jenny Soo Chin likewise were uncertain of the identification. But circumstantial evidence, when there is enough of it and it is good enough, can be just as damning and just as convicting as direct evidence, and the circumstantial evidence here was just that.

There were, of course, two witnesses who could have rung the final knell, whose testimony alone could well have been enough to convict Nash. But Alberto Torres, the superintendent on West Forty-fifth Street, had a very serious lapse of memory. He could remember nothing, he knew nothing, he had seen nothing; in fact, he said, he hadn't even been in New York on the evening of the murders. And Henry Oestericher knew nothing about the murders or about Nash. All he knew were stories about Margaret Barbera and the very bad things she had done to his friend and client Irwin Margolies. It would

172

have been nice to have had their real stories. But even without them, there was little hope for Nash.

There was now no question that Nash was the shooter. But there still was the major question: Who had supplied the gun and aimed it? As the evidence against Nash mounted, so, too, did the indications that the man who had bought and paid him had to be Irwin Margolies, despite the original convictions that white-collar criminals just don't do such things. Going through Nash's telephone records, the cops came up with a series of calls, from December until March, from Nash's phone or from Dane's, which Nash used frequently, to Oestericher's private office number. Some of those calls were made when Oestericher was not in residence, but when Margolies was using that office as his own. Some of those calls made while Oestericher was there to answer were followed almost immediately by calls from Oestericher to numbers where Margolies was known to be. All circumstantial, of course. What was needed was a direct link between Nash and Margolies, but unless Oestericher decided that truth was the better part of valor, it didn't then seem likely that they would come up with one.

There were other directions to go, certainly, with regard to the jeweler. He was, even after the murder of Barbera, still proclaiming his innocence in the matter of the Candor-Maguire fraud, still asserting that it had all been Barbera's doing, that she had stolen the jewelry and the cash, that she had master-minded and carried out the swindle without his knowledge, that he was an innocent victim of her scheming, and that her murder must have been the result of some private peccadillo of which he knew nothing. If he was concerned that something might emerge to tie him directly to Nash, he gave no sign.

What would have helped, certainly with the fraud investigation, were the Candor books that Barbera had made away with and hidden. One of Jenny Soo Chin's relatives told police that Barbera had stored a suitcase she said contained very important records in the Chin garage in Teaneck. But a few weeks before Chin's abduction and murder, Barbera had retrieved the case. It had not been seen since. The constant and thorough

173

searches of Barbera's apartment had failed to uncover it or any records, though much else had been found and gone through, mostly of a private nature not relating to her work at Candor.

Where, then, to look? Barbera had a safety-deposit box. Perhaps the records might be there along with, if Margolies was telling the truth, some of the diamonds and cash. A search warrant was obtained. John Wales went out to a Chemical Bank branch in Queens and served it on a Saturday morning in late April. "The box," he says, "was empty. That was the big joke. I went out and hid it myself, with millions of dollars in diamonds missing, and it was empty. I came back and I said to the captain, 'I hid that box.' He said, 'How did everything go?' I said, 'Well, I'm retiring very shortly.' "

But Chartrand had better luck. He had interviewed Barbera's brother and sister several times. "And while I'm talking to Margaret's sister, Faith, Faith tells me that there were some business records that the family removed from the apartment. And I said, 'What did they look like?' She said, 'Well, my brother's got them. They had a company name on them. They were big portfolios.' So I went to the loving brother and I asked him if this was so, and he said, 'Yes.' And I asked him if it would be possible for me to have them. He then says, 'I must talk to our attorney.' "

Barbera's family soon after the murder retained William Kunstler, the well-known and controversial attorney, to represent them in the suit they intended to bring against the federal government for failing to protect their sister.

"So," says Chartrand, "I called William and I told him who I am and I tell him what I've been told and I ask him if I could have them. He calls me back and says, 'The family says you may come and get them.' They turned out to be the true and accurate records of the Candor Diamond Corporation. They were examined by federal experts and the district attorney's accountants. And they pictured the entire fraud on paper by figures. And so now Mr. Margolies is going to hit the jackpot. He is going to have very great problems with the income-tax people and he is going to have very great problems with the fraud

174

people and we are going to put him on ice for a while and make sure he does not decide to run away again while we continue to look for more."

Then more began to surface. John Wales found the first possible direct link between Margolies and Nash that anybody on the official side knew about. Wales was moonlighting one weekend, doing some siding work on the house of a friend, a former FBI agent turned private investigator. In the middle of the afternoon, Wales took a break. He and his friend sat down, had a beer, and did some light reminiscing about police work, swapping tall stories, always trying to one-up each other. After a time, the friend asked Wales what he was working on. Wales said, "The CBS thing."

"Oh, yeah," the friend said. "I worked on that, or at least part of it."

"Sure," Wales said. "What did you do?"

"Then he started telling me about him and his son," Wales says. "They were doing some investigating for John P. Maguire and they were supposed to tail this guy Margolies and see if they could find out what he had done with the money. So one day they followed him into a building in midtown and they saw him have a meeting with a guy in the lobby. He said the guy looked like a hoodlum. That's how he described him. Only the description was Nash. The description fit Nash. Just Margolies and Nash. That was the one tie-in we could come up with at that time."

It was a beginning.

New York State, in the guise of the Manhattan district attorney and, in particular, Assistant District Attorney Gregory Waples, concentrated on Nash. For the investigators in Midtown North, in the task force, Waples was an unknown quantity. Another assistant district attorney, Donald Sullivan, had been handling the case from its inception, but he had been offered a better job and was seriously considering it, both from a professional and a personal standpoint. "He called me one day," Chartrand remembers, "and asked me to stop by, and we had lunch together. Lunch with Sullivan is a sandwich and a container of juice in the park behind the courthouse. He told me that he had been offered a spot as a bureau chief and he wanted the job. But he said that if he thought the selection of his replacement was not the guy to handle this thing, or for whatever reason, he would not agree to it and he would decline. And he talked about this with some of the high mucky-mucks in the DA's office. And a day later, he told me he spoke to the guy who was going to take over and he said he wanted me to come down and meet him. That's when I first met Greg Waples. I had never heard of Greg Waples until then. Greg Waples was a conservative-type person, but very, very competent in preparing. He did his homework. He didn't miss a trick. He played both sides, played the devil's advocate and was able to anticipate in many cases some of the moves of the other side. A good person and a good DA, and he's what we call they've got hidden down there and they pull them out when they need them." Armed with the massive circumstantial evidence the cops had gathered on Nash, Waples went before the grand jury and, in June 1982, emerged with an indictment of Nash for five murders—Jenny Soo Chin, Margaret Barbera, Leo Kuranuki, Robert Schulze, and Edward Benford.

Meanwhile, the federal government took out after Irwin and Madeleine Margolies for the Candor-Maguire fraud. Everybody agreed that the case, the still-incomplete case, against Margolies for murder must necessarily wait until after Nash's trial. First things first. And so, possessed of the books that detailed the scheme to defraud Maguire and the Internal Revenue Service and to enrich the Margolieses, the U.S. attorney for the Southern District of New York, in the persons of Assistant U.S. Attorneys Ira Block and Stephen Schlessinger, went before the federal grand jury that had been empaneled and that, once, had expected to hear the testimony of Margaret Barbera. When they emerged, they had won a wide-ranging indictment, of Margolies and his wife, charging them with over fifty counts of mail fraud, wire fraud, and interstate transportation of stolen property, to which would be added, a little later, additional counts charging personal and corporate income-tax evasion.

They were released on $75,000 bail each after Margolies posted a $200,000 personal-appearance bond secured by his Green-burgh home, a bond that was accepted even though there was some question as to just who owned the home now that the courts had ruled that the mortgage payment actually was made with money Candor, and Margolies, had stolen from Maguire and so was not a legal payment. But just to make sure that Irwin and Madeleine Margolies didn't take it into their heads to make another sudden trip to Israel or someplace else, the court put a travel restriction on them, limiting their movements to West-chester County, the Bronx, and Manhattan.

22

Between indictments and scheduled trials, there stretched, as always in the American system of justice, long months and much work. Irwin and Madeleine Margolies, free on bail, were docketed to face their peers in federal court in Manhattan in December 1982, on the multiple charges of fraud and tax evasion. They had a new lawyer now, an experienced criminal and civil attorney named Gary Woodfield. It was not that Margolies no longer trusted Oestericher. That trust went deep, especially as Oestericher was so intimately involved in all that Margolies had done; it went as deep as their long friendship. It was that Margolies knew all too well Oestericher's limitations as an attorney, and he was not about to put his fate and his future, nor those of his wife, in Oestericher's hands.

Donald Nash, languishing in the Manhattan House of Detention, his twenty-day cloning sentence served and now sitting in a cell without bail, would go before his peers in New York State Supreme Court in April 1983, a year after the shooting on Pier Ninety-two, on five counts of murder. His attorney, Lawrence Hochheiser, well known in criminal-law circles, paid a fee in excess of $15,000 by Scott Malen from the Margolies fund, had complained bitterly of foot-dragging, of unconscionable delays in the trial because the prosecution still hadn't amassed all its evidence and so Nash was being denied his right to a speedy trial. But a trial within a year was the norm, and Hochheiser knew it.

This was a time, then, for the prosecutions, both state and federal, to seek out even more damning evidence than they already had, time to organize that evidence into cases with no holes, and it was a time for the defense, of the Margolieses and of Nash, to try desperately to find the holes through which their clients could escape.

During those months, Nash was constantly in and out of his cell. He was ordered to appear for blood tests, to see if his blood matched any of the samples found in the van. He was ordered to appear to have samples of his hair taken, to see if it matched any of the hair found in the van. He was ordered to appear for test after test. He was taken to the district attorney's office for interviews, and there he sat silently beside his lawyer, refusing to answer any questions, refusing to say anything, refusing to implicate anyone.

"I removed Donald Nash from prison a number of times," Chartrand says. "On one occasion I took him from detention, and he was a very popular chap in jail. You've got to respect a man like this, what they were charging him with. And a guy said, 'We'll see you later, Don.' And Nash turned around and he pointed his finger as though it was a pistol and fired it. They practically idolized him there."

The evidence the government had put together against Irwin and Madeleine Margolies was very distressing to Woodfield when he went through it, and he became increasingly gloomy about their prospects. Their only hope, he came to realize, was to strike some sort of deal with the federal attorneys, to plea-bargain and, perhaps, win some kind of leniency. At the beginning, when this was only a simple fraud case, only a matter of missing money and gems, when there was still dispute over the evidence and culpability was open to doubt, the government might well have been interested, and, in exchange for a plea of guilty and the return of some of the loot, the Margolieses might have gotten off with a fine, a short vacation, and some harsh words. But Jenny Soo Chin and Margaret Barbera, and the three CBS technicians, still had been alive then. Times and the situation had changed radically. The government was convinced it could go to trial and win a conviction on most if not all of the counts in the indictments. All a plea bargain would do, then, was save some time and expense. So the government was in a position to hold firm, to bargain hard, to give almost nothing. For Irwin Margolies, Woodfield was told, there would be no deals. For Madeleine Margolies, just maybe, but that would depend on Irwin.

The lawyer explained it all to his clients. If the government pushed ahead and gained the convictions it so confidently expected, and then filed a harsh sentencing memorandum with the judge, in essence asking for the maximum sentences for the couple, then Irwin could face up to 250 years in prison and Madeleine not much less. Even with time off for good behavior, even if they served only the minimum one third of their sentences, neither Irwin Margolies, at forty-seven, nor Madeleine Margolies, at forty, could ever expect to see the outside world again, all their assets would be seized, and their children would be left destitute. And if the government was put through the time and expense of a trial, they could expect the worst.

The potential price of continued resistance, then, explained again and again by their lawyer, and the frigid atmosphere that hung over their meetings with their prosecutors, eventually convinced the Margolieses that they had little choice but to take whatever the government was prepared to offer and hope for the best. Early in November, the deal was struck.

Irwin Margolies, still maintaining that he was the innocent victim of an evil and untrustworthy employee, Margaret Barbera, agreed to plead guilty to fifty-one of the sixty-two counts of mail fraud, wire fraud, interstate transportation of stolen property, and personal and corporate tax evasion brought against him. He was doing so, he said, to protect his wife. In exchange, the government agreed to drop all the fraud charges against Madeleine Margolies, thereby allowing her to continue her attempts to retain possession of her Greenburgh home, her Florida condominium, and other assets, and accept only a guilty plea to five counts of tax evasion.

Even with their pleas, the couple was warned to expect little mercy. In accordance with Justice Department policy, the prosecutors made no recommendations as to what sentences they would like. But the memoranda filed with Judge John M. Cannella in Federal Court left no doubt as to the government's desires and expectations. There were two. One, running to sixty-one pages, detailed the Candor scheme to defraud Maguire and others. The second, filed as a secret supplement and held in confidence, went through the murders of Jenny Soo Chin and Margaret Barbera and what the government claimed was Irwin Margolies's role in them.

"The impact of the Margolieses' fraud," the government document said, "goes well beyond the mere misappropriation of many millions of dollars. Partly as a result of the monetary losses incurred, and other unfortunate consequences of the victimization, Maguire, a long-established and highly regarded name in the factoring world, will cease operations and be merged into another Irving Trust Company subsidiary. . . .

"So, too, the careers of several Maguire officers who were involved in the administration of the Candor account and who were themselves hoodwinked by the multifarious lies and other stratagems of the defendants have been crippled. Additionally, the Margolieses have left behind them a trail of creditors stretching from New York to London and then again to Israel.

"The effect of this fraud upon the financial community is more difficult to gauge. Commercial financing companies such as Maguire are an important industry in New York City, and the services they provide are essential to numerous other enterprises both in this community and elsewhere. A scheme of the dimension and notoriety as that committed by these defendants inevitably inhibits the growth of such companies and makes them more reluctant to offer their services to newer and small clients who may be precisely the enterprises which most need their assistance.

"Despite the devastating effects of their fraud upon institutions and individuals alike, defendants have done absolutely nothing to atone for their crimes. All requests for their cooperation have been rebuffed. . . . They have made no restitution nor have they so much as offered an explanation as to why restitution cannot be made. Indeed, defendants have tried every imaginable means to conceal their booty and to insulate it from the Government and their legions of creditors. . . . The conclusion is therefore inescapable that Irwin and Madeleine Margolies remain in jealous possession of many millions of dollars of stolen money and are confident that their sentences will not be such as to cause them to disgorge it. Indeed, their silence in this regard can only be taken as an indication of continuing criminal intent.

"Likewise, despite repeated entreaties from the Government, defendants have declined to assist in the continuing investigation of other persons who necessarily must have been involved in the fraud, except, of course, to thrust responsibility for Maguire's loss upon Margaret Barbera and Jenny Soo Chin, whom they know cannot refute their accusations. They have steadfastly declined to provide information concerning other crimes which have come to light over the course of the investigation. Significantly, at no time have they claimed that they lack information with which to cooperate in the ongoing investigation. Their complete intransigence in these matters must weigh heavily in their sentences. . . .

"The litany of their various activities over the long course of this scheme reads like an encyclopedia of fraud, deceit, and duplicity. Wrongful appropriation of funds by Mr. and Mrs. Margolies certainly was not undertaken out of any compelling human need. . . . Their business afforded them an ability to make an honest living and enjoy a most comfortable life. Rather, the only explanation for their conduct is that they were motivated by greed. . . . Given the magnitude of the crimes, the total lack of remorse or restitution, and the defendants' continuing avariciousness, vindication of the principles of specific and general deterrence requires the imposition of substantial sentences of imprisonment. It is apparent from all the available evidence and from the defendants' massive theft that they did not believe they would be caught, or, alternatively, that they concluded that the amounts of money involved were worth the risk. Unless the Court imposes sentences commensurate with the crime, the sad fact will be that their evaluation was correct."

Despite these harsh words, the government still was willing to waive the fraud charges against Madeleine Margolies and allow her to plead guilty to the tax-evasion ones only. "Undeniably," it said, "it is the case that of the two defendants, Irwin Margolies is far more culpable than his wife. However . . . Mrs. Margolies was an active participant in the Maguire fraud. To the extent that the Government's acceptance of guilty pleas from Mrs. Margolies to tax offenses only may seem inconsistent . . . ultimately the Government determined to accept guilty pleas from Mrs. Margolies to five tax felonies carrying aggregate prison terms of 19 years and fines totaling $35,000 because of our belief that such maximum penalties would provide this Court with an appropriate sentencing range with respect to all of Mrs. Margolies's criminal activity. . . . Although Mrs. Margolies can be said to be less culpable than her husband, in large measure this derives from his several and continuous efforts to protect her—to the fullest extent possible from direct and collateral consequences of conviction. Thus, earlier in these proceedings, Irwin Margolies represented to the Court that he wished to testify exculpatorily for his wife at a severed trial, and in his plea allocution, he sought to minimize her role in Candor's day-to-day operations. When all is said and done, however, the simple truth is that Madeleine Margolies played a vital and significant, although supporting, role in the Candor-Maguire crimes."

As for Irwin Margolies: "The Court, in fashioning an ap-

183

propriate sentence for Irwin Margolies, should give full consideration to his responsibility for the murder of at least one prospective Government witness and the disappearance through violence of another. If persuaded of Mr. Margolies's direct connection with these heinous acts, the punishment which the Court would otherwise impose upon Margolies should then be enhanced to reflect his responsibility for these most ultimate acts of obstruction of justice."

Judge Cannella read the memoranda and reached his decision. On December 1, 1982, he sentenced Irwin Margolies to 28 years in federal prison and fined him $72,000. "I am satisfied," the judge said, "that there is no real remorse in this defendant at this time. He feels it's like paying rent for a loft. I believe that after serving his sentence, the fruits of his crime will still be there for him." The judge then added that he hoped the Manhattan district attorney would take additional and appropriate action against Margolies if he found sufficient evidence to bring him to trial for murder. But the twenty-eight years for fraud was the longest term ever handed down in New York for a white-collar crime. Judge Cannella ordered Margolies remanded to prison without delay, and the once and still millionaire jeweler was shackled and led off a few blocks to the federally run Metropolitan Correctional Center, the first stop on a long journey, the place where he would remain until the authorities decided where he would go next.

Three days later, it was Madeleine Margolies's turn to face Judge Cannella. She was tearful, contrite. "I relied on my husband's advice on anything I may have done," she said, sobbing. To which federal attorney Ira Block retorted sarcastically, "One would have to accept the fact that Mrs. Margolies lived in a cocoon." Judge Cannella heard her out and then sentenced her to three years in a federal prison, which meant she would be eligible for parole in a year, and fined her $35,000. He gave her until late January to get her affairs in order before beginning that sentence.

An aerial view of Keansburg, New Jersey, with Donald Nash's home indicated by arrow. Police feared that the swamp area might contain another
body.

The living room in the Nash home.

The garage attached to the Nash home in which Nash's van was repainted.

N.Y.P.D.

Police frogmen search the tidal creek behind the Nash home. Five .22 cartridges were discovered.

FORENSIC REPORT

PD321-091(4/72)   CRIME SCENE UNIT

25M-801091(75)

COMPLAINT NO.	PCT.	DETECTIVE DISTRICT	DATE OF REPORT	CRIME LAB NO. (IF ANY)	RUN NUMBER
10884	MTN	MTS PLU	4/23/82		82/989-E

OFFENSE	TIME NOTIFIED	TIME RESPONDED	TIME COMPLETED
Past homicides	4/22/82 0700	4/22/82 0900	4/22/82 2000

DATE & TIME OF OCCURRENCE	PLACE OF OCCURRENCE	APT/FLOOR
4/12/82 1815	KEANSBERG, NJ	

NAME OF ☐COMPLAINANT ☐DECEASED	SEX	COLOR	DATE OF BIRTH	ADDRESS	PHONE NO.

DEFENDANT'S NAME	ADDRESS	DATE OF BIRTH	ARREST NO.	"B" NUMBER

SUMMARY OF CASE

The undersigned investigators responded to KEANSBERG, NJ at the request of Det. R. BONAN, Manh. Met. Area Task Force to take a series of photographs of a house and garage in conjunction with an ongoing investigation. A search warrant was secured by the Red Bank, NJ FBI Office. P.O. Nick PETRAKO NYPD Crime Lab accompanied us to the scene and was present when the recovered evidence was turned over to the NYPD. All evidence was recovered, packaged, labelled and noted by the FBI before being delivered to NYPD.

FINGERPRINTS OR PHOTOGRAPHS NO. AREA/ITEM PROCESSED	AGENT/PROCEDURE USED	RESULTS NEG/POS.

PHOTOGRAPHS:

Photos 1 through 17: Exterior of garage, house, surrounding grounds and creek behind the house. All taken befrore any search was begun.

Photos 18 through 27: SCUBA team conducting search in creek behind the house and garage.

Photo 28: Evidence collection table, all evidence brought here to be labelled, packaged and noted.

Photo 29: Five (5) cal. .22LR cartridges found by SCUBA team in creek.

Photos 30 through 55: Interior of garage including hidden room. Photo no. 48 shows a discharged cal .22 LR shell on rear wall of garage.

Photos 56 through 73: Interior of house, family present while photos were taken.

NO. SCENE NEGATIVES:	BLACK/WHITE	COLOR	FINGERPRINT PHOTOS/NEGATIVES	ELIMINATIONS/SUSPECTS ☐YES ☐NO SEE OVER
VEHICLE EXAMINATION			NAME/ADDRESS OF OWNER	
	LICENSE NO.	ODOMETER		

The bedroom in Margaret Barbera's apartment.

The living room in Margaret Barbera's apartment.

FORENSIC REPORT

PD321-091(4/72)

29M-801091(75)

COMPLAINT NO.	PCT.	DETECTIVE DISTRICT	DATE OF REPORT	CRIME LAB NO. (IF ANY)	RUN NUMBER
10884	MTN	MTN-PDU	4/13/82		82-989 B

OFFENSE

	TIME NOTIFIED	TIME RESPONDED	TIME COMPLETED
Homicide (4)	0700	0730	1230

DATE & TIME OF OCCURRENCE   PLACE OF OCCURRENCE   APT/FLOOR

4/12/82 1815 hrs Pier # 92 & 12th Ave. (Responded to MTN-Pct Garage)

NAME OF ☐COMPLAINANT ☒DECEASED	SEX	COLOR	DATE OF BIRTH	ADDRESS	PHONE NO.
MARGARET BARBERA	F	W		631 Cumberland Ave. Teaneck N.J.	

DEFENDANT'S NAME   ADDRESS   DATE OF BIRTH   ARREST NO.   B. NUMBER

SUMMARY OF CASE

The undersigned investigator was requested to respond to MTN Pct. garage to process a 1981 BMW, registration 384 PVA (NJ).
The vehicle belonged to the deceased and was parked at the above location when the multiple homicides occurred. Close examination of the vehicle left front lock revealed that the perpetrator jammed the lock with small pieces of wood to lure the victim to the right side of the vehicle.
Based on the investigation the following crime scene services were performed:

FINGERPRINTS OR PHOTOGRAPHS

NO.	AREA/ITEM PROCESSED	AGENT/PROCEDURE USED	RESULTS NEG/POS.

FINGERPRINTS:

L1.	Dashboard gauges glass, right side	White Powder	Lifted/Pol.
L2.	Styroform coffee cup on dash	Black Powder	" "
L3.	Styroform coffee cup on dash	Black Powder	" "

PHOTOGRAPHS:

1.   General view of rear of vehicle
2.   General view of right side of vehicle exterior
3.   General view of right side of vehicle exterior from rear to front
4.   General view of left side of vehicle exterior
5.   Close-up view of right front interior of vehicle
6.   Close-up view of left front interior of vehicle
7.   Close-up view of rear interior of vehicle

NO. SCENE NEGATIVES.	BLACK/WHITE	COLOR		FINGERPRINT PHOTOS / NEGATIVES	ELIMINATIONS / SUSPECTS ☐YES ☐NO SEE OVER
7	7	10		Pol	

VEHICLE EXAMINATION   NAME / ADDRESS OF OWNER

YEAR	MAKE	LICENSE NO.	ODOMETER	MARGARET BARBERA (Dec)
81	BMW (Blue)	384 PVA (NJ)	13829	631 Cumberland St. Teaneck N.J.

SAFE EXAMINATION - TYPE   HOW OPENED   TRACE MATERIAL COLLECTED

N/A

OTHER EVIDENCE   LOCATION   DISPOSITION

RANK / NAME ASSIGNED DETECTIVE	SHIELD	COMMAND	RANK / NAME TECHNICIAN & ASSISTANT	SHIELD
Det. Chartrand		MTN-PDU	P.O. Fernando Duran	10337
			Det. M. Kane	2825

A police design specialist at work drafting the scene of the murder of the three CBS employees.

Nash's repainted van with decals in custody of the Kentucky State Police.

The interior of Nash's van with newly purchased camping equipment.

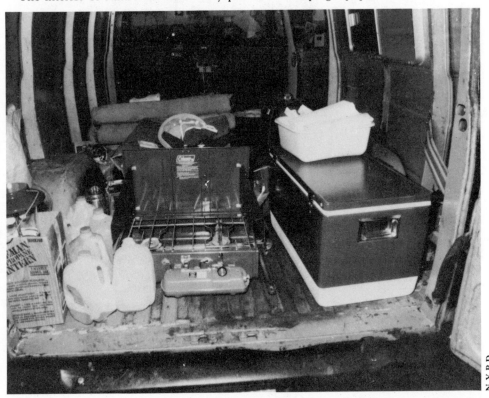

Madeleine and Irwin Margoles leaving Federal District Court.

23

Madeleine Margolies had a lot to do and not much time to do it. Sometime between Christmas and New Year's, she paid a call on family friend and still, in some things, adviser and attorney Henry Oestericher. With her she carried a wallet containing several hundred thousand dollars' worth of diamonds. Following Madeleine's orders, Oestericher walked up to Forty-seventh Street and paid a call on another Margolies friend and ally, jeweler Joseph Gubits. He handed the wallet with its horde of diamonds to Gubits and passed on Madeleine's instructions: Gubits was to protect those diamonds and, when ordered, turn them piece by piece into cash to be delivered to Madeleine's brother, Scott Malen, to Oestericher, or to some other trusted person, to take care of the Margolies family needs while she was away.

A few weeks later, she summoned her brother, who was then acting as president of Madeleine Chain. She gave him an envelope. In the envelope were $100 bills, $50,000 worth. He was to use the money to pay the expenses of running the Green-burgh house and taking care of Douglas and Steven Margolies, to pay lawyers, and to pass on to whomever else Madeleine or Irwin told him to pay.

And there were people to pay. Irwin Margolies did not like the Metropolitan Correctional Center one bit. He kept pro-testing his innocence, kept looking for ways to get out, and kept blaming a lot of other people for his troubles. If at anyone, his ire was directed at Maguire-Irving Trust attorney David Blejwas. If Blejwas hadn't been so dogged in his digging into the swindle, if Blejwas hadn't been so determined to put the onus on Mar-golies, it all would have blown away, the blame would have rested on Margaret Barbera, and Margolies would be free and guiltless. Margolies had tasted blood, even if only by proxy, and he had found the taste not unpalatable. He had come to believe that more blood, more murder, was the solution to all his prob-lems. Anyone who crossed him deserved to die. And that was particularly true of David Blejwas. Of course, Margolies would not stoop to doing such a deed himself. There were always others he could buy who would do it for him, and he had plenty of money to do the buying. It didn't matter that he was locked up in a cell. In fact, what better place to find a killer-for-hire than in a prison cell.

But, as a matter of fact, prison may be just the wrong place to look for a killer-for-hire, and especially the Metropolitan Correctional Center. As Chartrand says, "The feds and the federal marshals at MCC have an unlimited number of infor-mants in there. One floor is nothing but federal informants. I would say that a good number of the other floors have persons that are federal informants. And it was no time at all before friendly businessman Irwin is being suckered to death by the other inmates, the informers, the people on the staff. I don't know whether it's totally corrupt or not, but extras are always available if you have the wherewithal, and, of course, Irwin had the wherewithal. So he lived rather comfortably. Irwin liked his food, and so he ate reasonably well. And there were a couple of other obese chaps there who ate reasonably well, too, on

Irwin, because they promised to do good things for him and, of course, they had to be rewarded for doing those good things. But Irwin rarely discussed with them what he was doing and planning. With a very few exceptions."

It did not take very long before the word began to circulate on Margolies's floor at the Metropolitan Correctional Center that the jeweler was interested in putting a proposition to someone who might be interested in listening. The proposition entailed a little contract for some violence. As Chartrand says, "There were several maneuvers going on within the system as to who may be open to accept this contract. There were a number of people who were anxious to have this contract because this man stole five and a half million dollars, and there's got to be money out there he can control and get loose. So even if we don't do it, we can fuck him out of it and there's nothing he can do about it."

Among all those inmates looking for a piece of the Margolies action, two just happened to be his cellmates at various times during December and January. Both were career criminals, as people with long records are called these days. One was Henry Adair, who, though only in his early thirties, had been convicted of a variety of major crimes on ten different occasions and was then awaiting a transfer to a more permanent facility after a conviction for smuggling a boatload of narcotics and a sentence of twenty-five years. The other was Vincent Calise, a little older than Adair but his match when it came to a criminal past and present. Neither had any great desire to spend the rest of their good years on the inside. Both would do almost anything to get back on the outside.

Margolies whiled away the hours in his cell playing checkers and chess with Adair or Calise, and doing a lot of talking, about the unfairness of the criminal-justice system, and especially about the people on the outside who were responsible for putting him where he was. During these conversations, Margolies learned a lot about his cellmates, and the more he learned, the more he thought they were just the right guys for him. He made a proposition, to Adair and to Calise. And one after the other, they ran to the authorities. In exchange for a little courtesy and assistance, they said, they were willing to turn informant and wrap up Margolies for the authorities. The little courtesy and assistance they wanted, of course, was freedom and a new life as protected witnesses. It was not an uncommon arrangement, and there were few arguments. If they got what they promised, they would get what they asked.

Both were equipped with miniature tape recorders and wireless transmitters and, on different occasions when they shared the cell with him, sent back and told to engage Margolies in a little polite conversation. It was not a very difficult assignment. Margolies always was ready to talk to Adair or Calise about important things, such as hiring.

"I understand you're a magician," he told Adair on one occasion. "I understand you make people disappear. I want somebody to disappear permanently." Could Adair make this happen in a very professional manner?

Adair certainly could and, for the right price, would. Who was this person?

A lawyer named David Blejwas, Margolies said. How much did Adair charge for such a contract?

Adair threw out the figure of $15,000. Margolies did not quibble. Adair asked for some specifics about Blejwas so he would know how to reach him and recognize him. Margolies took out a piece of paper and wrote Blejwas's name, home and business address, employer's name, regular business hours, and a physical description. He supplemented that with a photograph of Blejwas he had clipped from a newspaper. What he truly desired, Margolies told Adair, was for Blejwas to get a bullet in the head. But it shouldn't be done from ambush, in the dark. Blejwas should know what was about to happen, and before he pulled the trigger, Adair should give him a message: "Let him know it's from Irv."

A face-to-face killing might be a little more difficult, Adair explained. Was Blejwas married? Did he have children? If so, they might get in the way.

Yes, Margolies said, Blejwas was married and had children,

but Adair shouldn't worry about that. "If they have to be taken care of," he said, "take care of them." And if it came to that, then Margolies would throw a little more into the pot to make up for Adair's additional trouble.

When Adair reported the conversation and proposal, and when the cops, federal and New York, heard the words, they immediately gave Blejwas around-the-clock protection until the danger finally passed.

With the contract agreed to, Margolies offered to make a down payment to Adair of $2,000, with the balance to be paid on delivery, though he didn't want Adair to make the delivery until Madeleine Margolies was out of prison, a year in the future. That was fine with Adair. He could report it all to the authorities, receive his part of their bargain with him, and Margolies would never be the wiser, unless and until Adair showed up in a courtroom to tell the world all about it. Still, Adair and the government wanted the down payment made to seal the deal. No problem for Margolies. All Adair had to do, he said, was send a friend or a messenger to Federal Express in Manhattan and Margolies would make sure that there was a package waiting for him. It would contain the money and a good photograph of Blejwas.

It was a simple thing for Margolies to get the word out and make all the arrangements. "Telecommunications in the MCC is no problem," Chartrand explains. "You have to work that out with the other inmates. If four of us are on a floor, along with eight others, and I am known to be the possessor of millions of dollars, I spread it around, give some to a guy to keep an eye on my back, give some to a guy to keep an eye on my front, and I give you some and you some and then we give some to the other fellows so I can keep the phone. There's only one phone on that particular tier, or on any tier, and I want to keep that phone free and open to me between, say, seven and seven-twelve every evening. Irwin laid it out. They all have it. You pay for a legitimate phone answering service and you pay them a monthly fee for an allocated amount of time, and if you go over, you've got to pay for that, too. And every night between seven and seven-twelve, Irwin calls his answering service and the person he wants to talk to calls the answering service and the connection is made through the answering service. This is particularly valuable when you want to talk to someone in another prison, because calls from one inmate in one prison to another inmate in a different prison are not allowed. This way, neither inmate is calling another prison directly. Irwin and Madeleine did this all the time, every night, once she went away. If you have the money or the influence or the sock, you can have the particular time frame on the phone and that time frame is yours and nobody else can use it because you are paying for it. So Irwin had it every day."

Margolies called Madeleine. He gave her instructions. She had to hurry because she was about to leave for prison herself. She hurried. On January 20, the day before she was to depart, she gave her brother, Scott Malen, a package. It contained twenty $100 bills, $2,000, and a very good photograph of David Blejwas. Later that day, Malen delivered the package to Federal Express, and very soon it was picked up by the messenger from Adair.

The deal complete, the government informed that the connection had been established, the bargain was kept. Adair walked out of the prison, a free man. He went to his friend, picked up his package, went to the FBI and handed it over, minus $200 that he kept for himself to pay for his trouble.

But Adair wasn't through. He was, after all, now a government informant, and he owed it to his new employers to keep them up to date on Margolies's plans, to supply them with plenty of information. So when Margolies called, he answered, and less than two weeks after he walked out of the Metropolitan Correctional Center, he walked back in. Only this time it was not as a prisoner. This time he carried credentials that identified him as Irwin Margolies's paralegal associate counsel, which gave him not only visiting privileges but also a nice private unbugged room to have a chat with Margolies in. Of course, it wasn't quite unbugged, or private, since Adair was nicely wired with a tape recorder. They talked about the contract. Margolies reiterated that Adair should wait to carry it out until Madeleine was a free

198

woman again. Margolies asked if Adair had received the package. Adair assured him he had. Then Adair complained about how hard things were on the outside, how difficult it was to get enough money to live. Margolies said that was no problem. If Adair dropped around to see his brother-in-law, there might be a little envelope with some expense money waiting for him. Adair went to the offices of Madeleine Chain. The receptionist, indeed, had an envelope waiting for him. Adair thanked her, put the envelope in his pocket, hurried off to the FBI, and handed it to Special Agent John Truslow. Truslow opened it. Inside were five new $100 bills.

There was still more for Adair to do. Over the next few weeks, he spoke to Malen several times by phone, receiving messages from Margolies, had a direct telephone conversation with Margolies through the answering service hookup, and, in response to a Margolies request, agreed to drop by the Metropolitan Correctional Center again for another session of private paralegal-client conversation. That meeting was a rehash of the previous one, though during it Margolies assured Adair that any time he needed money, Malen would have it waiting for him. Indeed, Malen did, on several other occasions, passing on envelopes containing $100 or $200 at a time, envelopes that, naturally, Adair handed over to Truslow.

But Adair had a problem. He had never been able to stay out of trouble, had never been able to resist the chance for the big score if somebody presented him with one. Usually those chances led to a little time at public expense. Now, even with freedom and the start of a new life and a new chance, when a friend came to Adair with a proposition, Adair just couldn't turn it down. He took a little trip out of the country, and on the way back, the federal authorities were waiting for him. He was, it seems, carrying a bundle, and in the bundle was a lot of hashish. The federal agents took the hashish and put Adair back into a cell. His time on the outside was over, his career as a government informant was at an end, and, even with the tapes he had made, he was left with little credibility as a witness against Margolies.

199

Adair, though, was not the only inmate with whom Margolies was bargaining and handing out contracts. There was his other cellmate, Vincent Calise. Calise, if Margolies had his way, would be a backup in case something happened to Adair. And Calise would have a few jobs of his own to do for Margolies, because Margolies thought that not just Blejwas should be dead but others as well. There was an automobile dealer out on Long Island who, Margolies was sure, had screwed him when the jeweler had bought one of his cars. Nobody, of course, screwed Irwin Margolies and lived. And there was U.S. Assistant Attorney Ira Block who, Margolies declared, was "a very evil person who should be shot in the head." How much would Calise want for doing these jobs, and backing up Adair, when Calise got out of jail?

Calise was no cheapskate. He wanted $50,000, with $20,000 up front. His intention, he assured federal agents who were listening to the negotiations, was never to do the job but "to take the $20,000 and put it in my pocket."

Unfortunately for Calise, the government, and Margolies, somebody who shouldn't have been listening was listening. Calise was wearing a wireless transmitter, sending the conversation back to agents. But down at the end of the cellblock, another prisoner happened to be listening to the radio. "He had one of those exquisite radios that he wasn't supposed to have but he had it," Chartrand says. "The guy kept changing his channels and in doing so, he's hearing Irwin at the other end of the corridor holding a very confidential conversation. And, of course, he ran right back and told him, 'I got you on my radio. I listened to you.' "

So ended the bargaining with Vincent Calise, and so ended Calise's visions of a new life on the outside. His twenty-five-year term for narcotics smuggling stood, unchanged.

Margolies, of course, had more on his mind than just arranging to have Blejwas, Block, and a car dealer murdered. He was very concerned about the well-being of his wife once she was shipped down to the Federal Prison for Women at Alderson, W. Va. She didn't like it at all. She didn't like the accommodations. She didn't like the terrible food, not only was it inedible, it also wasn't kosher. She didn't like being treated like a criminal. And she was particularly distressed with becoming the object of homosexual assaults. She would later claim, in a suit filed against the federal government, that on the day she arrived at Alderson, another inmate grabbed her, threw her against a wall, and began to fondle and otherwise molest her, declaring, "Welcome, Little Miss Rich Bitch, I want to give you a taste of what it's like." She managed to break free, but then blacked out and fainted. That was just the beginning, she said. The assaults continued uninterrupted and "every day was a challenge to survive." The place "was like a horror movie . . . made up of junkies, lesbians, and bull dykes fondling each other, tongue-kissing, and making sexual advances."

"It did not come as any surprise to anybody, either in the FBI or us," Chartrand says. Indeed, there was some cynical observation that not only were Madeleine Margolies's prison experiences no surprise, but also they were precisely what had been expected and hoped for. If things got too difficult for her at Alderson, then just maybe she might decide to make another deal, lay out for the authorities everything she knew about Irwin, including what she knew about his part in the murders of Jenny Soo Chin and Margaret Barbera, in exchange for a quick release and the comforts of home on the outside.

But Margolies himself was not unaware of that possibility. His wife called him, or he called her, through the answering services every night, and he heard her tales of woe. He did what he could to change her situation. He arranged for money to be sent down so that she could have a private table at meals and have kosher food. "Irwin paid," Chartrand reports, "a sizable amount of money to have Madeleine removed from the general population and to have Madeleine treated more in the manner to which she was accustomed. And he made other arrangements. Another inmate convinced him that he had a sister in that particular correctional facility who would look after Madeleine and protect her from all those bad people. And Irwin went to the well again. And another fellow convinced Irwin that he could help Madeleine transfer to a much nicer place. And Irwin went along with that story as well. Irwin was very concerned about his wife. And he did all these things to help her and to make sure that she was as comfortable and loyal as a wife should be. And she was very loyal and while she was a prisoner she did not say anything to incriminate Irwin. But, of course, Irwin could never be sure and there came a time when he put out an exploratory contract on her. It never came to anything, but he explored it."

24

The People of the State of New York v. *Donald Nash,* charged with four counts of murder in the second degree and one count of conspiracy to commit murder, opened before Justice Clifford A. Scott and a jury of nine men and three women in Supreme Court in Manhattan on March 31, 1983. Before it ended, nearly two months later, Assistant District Attorney Gregory Waples, without a single eyewitness who could point to Nash and declare positively, "I saw him do it," deluged the court with testimony from 127 witnesses bolstered by more than 380 individual pieces of evidence and exhibits, a torrent of circumstantial evidence that would, he was sure, negate the need for the witness he lacked, would be potent enough to drown Nash.

The presentation was neat and orderly, or as neat and orderly as is possible in a court of law. Waples proved conclusively that four people were dead and probably a fifth, and that those four people, and probably the fifth, had been murdered by bullets to the head from a .22-caliber weapon. That was, of course, the essential preliminary. Without death, without the showing that the death was caused by another person, was murder, there could be no indictment and no trial. Everyone might know it, but the prosecution still must prove it. Angelo Sicca told how he had seen the murders of his fellow CBS technicians, how he had seen the shooter dragging the limp body of a woman, Margaret Barbera, around a silver van, how he himself had fled in fear and then returned and summoned help. What he could not do was describe the killer. "I didn't want to make eye contact. . . . I wasn't trying to study this man. I was trying to get out of there."

Robert Schlop, the next CBS technician to appear on the scene, talked about stumbling over the bodies a little after the murders, though he had not seen them, had not seen the silver van, had not seen the killer. But he did remember that, a week earlier, he had seen a silver van on the pier and had brushed against its driver who was hurrying to it. The driver he remembered clearly. He pointed to the defense table, to Donald Nash, and positively identified him as that driver.

Manuel Infante, the artist-bartender, related his early-morning stroll with his dog through the side streets and alleys of lower Manhattan, a stroll that ended when the dog sniffed out the body of Margaret Barbera.

Lieutenant Dick Gallagher tied Margaret Barbera to the pier as he told of hearing the report of the discovery of the body, of rushing down to Franklin Alley with the shoes found on the pier and discovering that the shoes were a perfect fit.

There were the Ridgewood teenagers who had witnessed the abduction of Jenny Soo Chin, had heard her scream as a man in a ski mask came up behind her and shoved her into her car and then drove away on a dark January night. But their descriptions of the man varied and were not consistent, and they could not point to Nash, or anyone, and say he was that man. Then cops told how, days later, they discovered Jenny Soo Chin's abandoned car on Manhattan's West Side and in it bloodstains and a spent .22-cartridge shell casing.

If they could say nothing, then, to identify the man who

had done these things, or even if the same man had done them all, these witnesses, nevertheless, established clearly that initial and fateful premise: Crimes had been committed, four murders had been done, a fifth person had been kidnapped and probably murdered. Still, except for Schlop, who had seen Nash on the pier a week before the murders, there was nothing yet to tie the defendant to the crimes.

That would come with a platoon of New York cops, Kentucky State troopers, FBI agents, and expert witnesses of all kinds filling the courtroom with the details of the long investigation, of tracking down leads, of scientific tests, and a lot more, all pointing directly to Donald Nash as the killer, as the man who had done all these deeds.

The jury heard, in the jargon of the police and the language of the scientist and in everyday words, about the parking application with its attempt to deceive filed at Pier Ninety-two and how John Wales had traced it back to Donald Nash; about Nash's van spotted in Barbera's neighborhood and the calls from that neighborhood charged to Nash's phone, and other calls charged to the Nash phone; about the discovery of shell casings, on the pier, in Jenny Soo Chin's car, in the van, in Nash's garage, in the creek behind his home, and elsewhere, all fired from the same gun; about the purchase of ammunition by Nash; about bloodstains and whose they were and where they had been found; about a van being repainted; about a lost parking ticket at Newark Airport and its discovery in the van; about a chase from New Jersey to Kentucky; about arrest and more and more. The testimony and the exhibits washed across the courtroom in a flood, day by day, week by week, to the point where there were some who thought Waples was going in for overkill. But his case was circumstantial; he had no witness who could positively place Nash on the scene of the murders at the moment they happened, who had seen Nash pull the trigger. And so Waples was not one to leave anything to chance; he would miss no possibilities, would leave no air holes for Nash to find and rise to the surface.

If there was drama and surprise, it came with the appearance as prosecution witnesses, testifying under grants of immunity, of Nash's nephews, Robert and Thomas Dane, and of his common-law wife of nearly two decades, Jeanne Nash. Much of their testimony was given with reluctance, dragged from them by the battering of Waples, who treated them not as his own friendly witnesses but as hostile adversaries. And that testimony was devastating to Donald Nash.

Robert Dane was led through the abandoning of his silver van in the Bronx, its license plate and one tire removed, on the day that just happened to follow the disappearance of Jenny Soo Chin. He knew nothing about that, of course. He had ditched the van only so he could collect $6,000 in insurance, and he was surprised and appalled when the van was recovered and turned back to him.

"Isn't it a fact," Waples demanded, "that on January 5, you loaned the van to your brother, Thomas, and your uncle?"

"No," replied Robert Dane.

"Isn't it a fact," Waples continued, "that on January 5, when you received the van back, you were informed that something had happened with the van?"

"No."

"Wasn't it suggested to you that you'd better get rid of the van and that's why you took it to the Bronx?"

"No." It was only a coincidence, a strange one, Dane insisted, that the van and the disappearance of Jenny Soo Chin so closely coincided. He knew nothing about that and had had nothing to do with it.

The jury is supposed to believe that, Waples said sarcastically, when it is a fact, isn't it, that Dane filed a false report, a criminal offense, with his insurance company about the van, and that he lied to the insurance company?

Dane admitted that he had done this criminal thing, that he had lied, but nevertheless he was telling the truth now.

If Waples, then, was, at the very least, accusing Robert Dane of being an accessory after the fact to the murder of Jenny Soo Chin—for which, having been granted immunity in exchange for his testimony, he would not be tried even if any solid evidence could be found—he went even further with Dane's younger brother, Thomas.

"Isn't it a fact," Waples asked, though from his manner it was apparent that he was sure of the true answer, "that you conspired with Donald Nash to murder Jenny Soo Chin?"

"No."

"Did you conspire with Donald Nash to murder Margaret Barbera?"

"No, I did not."

Waples' disbelief was patent. He pressed on to show just how deeply Thomas Dane was involved with his uncle in these deeds, even if Thomas would never be brought to trial for that involvement. He asked Dane if he had ever seen a .22 automatic equipped with a silencer. Dane said he never had, except in the movies. But Waples moved forward, wrung from him the admission that he had made calls to suppliers of the parts for a silencer, had signed for the delivery of those parts, and had paid for them. But, he maintained, he had never opened the packages; he had done it all at the behest of Uncle Donald, and had handed the packages over to him unopened.

Waples let that hang. Then he asked if Dane had ever called Margaret Barbera at her unlisted home phone number in Queens. Dane was shocked. He had never done such a thing. Waples calmly produced telephone records that showed that just such a call had been placed from Dane's home phone. Reluctantly, Dane said that Uncle Donald often used that phone.

Had Dane ever spoken with Irwin Margolies? Never, Dane replied to Waples. Waples produced more telephone records, this time showing that a call had been made from Dane's phone to the private unlisted office number of attorney Henry Oestericher at a time when Margolies was using that office and phone. Dane had not made those calls, he insisted. And again he had to say that Uncle Donald used that phone often.

Waples kept asking, and the more he asked, the more he trapped Thomas Dane in a web of complicity that Dane could explain only by implicating his uncle ever more deeply. There was the night of the Pier Ninety-two murders and Dane's meeting with Nash, his following Nash to Newark Airport, his driving Nash back home, his shopping trips with Nash, his helping Nash paint the silver van black, his return to Newark Airport with Nash and the van, another shopping trip to buy camping equipment, another return to the airport when Nash retrieved the van once more and drove south.

All this, now, was different from the stories he had told the grand jury when it had looked into the murders. Was Dane telling the truth now? Yes, he said. Had he lied to the grand jury, then? Yes, Dane said. "I guess I was upset, nervous."

Still, Dane had some surprises for Waples that did not sit well with the prosecutor when Dane was recalled a few days after his initial ordeal on the witness stand. In the intervening period, detectives had appeared at Dane's home, had searched his attic, had come away with another .22-caliber shell casing, a casing that matched all the others. Waples wanted to know how Dane explained the fact that such a casing happened to be in his attic, in an otherwise empty attaché case.

Dane said he had no idea. He had never seen the casing before. "I have a feeling," he said, "it was put there. It definitely was not there before the police came. It's funny. I had a couple of dozen other boxes in the attic which were not touched." And, Dane added, Detectives Richie Bohan and Augie Sanchez, who had done the searching and found the casing, did not seem at all surprised when they found it, and they did not even take precautions to save any fingerprints it might have contained.

Dane had another little shock, and it came when Lawrence Hochheiser, Nash's lawyer, took over to do some cross-examining. Hochheiser treated Dane a lot more sympathetically and gently than had Waples and asked Dane if he had had a visit and a discussion with one of the detectives.

Yes, Dane said. Augie Sanchez had taken him aside and suggested that he ought to pay a little visit to his uncle in jail and persuade his uncle that he "should not be taken advantage of . . . he should help the police clear this whole matter up and settle things." There was Jenny Soo Chin. Dane, if he didn't already know, should find out from Uncle Donald what he had

208

done with her and where her body was so that she could get a decent burial. That would make her family feel a lot better. And, Sanchez said, it was obvious that Nash was going to go away for a very long time, so why should he keep his mouth closed and go on protecting "that fat Jew bastard"? Dane ought to think very hard about that and talk to his uncle, because Dane was "a very lucky boy, breathing fresh air. You should be in jail with your uncle."

(After Dane's revelation, Sanchez was asked about the story. He shrugged it off. He had talked to Dane, yes, had said much of what Dane related but, he said, he had never called Irwin Margolies "fat," even though the man was rather obese. Sanchez, a tough, pugnacious, and, to some, a frightening figure, might dismiss it as nonsense, not worth commenting about, but it left a very bad taste in the mouths of others.)

Then there was the pathetic figure of Jeanne Nash. "Don is not a violent man," she insisted in a shaking, tear-filled voice. "He is not a murderer. There is no way Don could have been on that pier and shot those people. There is a mistake somewhere. Don is loved by everyone. He never turned a favor down."

Waples was gentle toward her, but he got from her what he had called her to get. She admitted that Nash had called her at home "a little bit after six" on the evening of the murders and told her to go over to Thomas Dane's house and tell him to get off the phone because it was important for Nash to speak to him.

In his opening remarks, Waples had said he would show not only that Donald Nash had committed these crimes but also that he had been hired to commit them and that the man who had hired him was Irwin Margolies, in a desperate attempt to cover up his fraud and keep his wealth. Waples never showed it. Though Margolies's name was mentioned now and again in testimony, there was no real evidence to link the two men. If Waples had no more than what he had revealed during this trial, then, some legal experts said, maybe Nash would take the fall, but he would take it alone. They had heard nothing that could possibly be used to bring Margolies to trial, or even to indict him.

The case against Nash, then, seemed overwhelming, if circumstantial. Hochheiser was in an almost hopeless position in any attempt to defend his client. He got little or no cooperation from Nash. "Either out of love or fear," Hochheiser said, "he seems reluctant, he seems unwilling to authorize the most vigorous kind of defense." The only witness Hochheiser could come up with to testify for Nash was an ophthalmologist, whose contribution was to say that Nash was blind in one eye and had very limited sight in the other. To Hochheiser, this meant there was no way Nash could have aimed a pistol and shot four people. Waples had a very simple answer to that. When a gun is put against somebody's head, or held within a few inches of the target, even a blind man becomes a sharpshooter.

What could Hochheiser say to the jury, in closing, to try to win those nine men and three women, to wean them from the state's case? That case, he said, was purely circumstantial, and "if you start with the presumption of innocence, then it does not fit, too much sticks out around the edges. . . . My client did not shoot anybody. My client did not kill anybody. They could call a thousand and fifty witnesses and he will still be innocent. Who is Donald Nash? A foolish man, but certainly not a murderer."

Waples derided that. "I don't have the answer to what snapped in the defendant's mind that transformed him from a human being to an amoral automaton who relentlessly pursued two women for months and remorselessly executed three CBS employees," he declared. "In this case, the circumstantial evidence is more convincing and more persuasive than direct evidence." And he tried, one last time, to bring Irwin Margolies into focus. "Candor," he said, "is the germ from which the pestilence of the crime grew. Irwin Margolies set in motion a chain of events that ultimately claimed the lives of five people."

But the jury was not there to judge Irwin Margolies. Its job was to judge the guilt or innocence of Donald Nash. It took thirteen hours of deliberation to decide that, the only sticking point in the minds of some of the jurors whether or not the police had planted that shell casing in Thomas Dane's attic. Aside from that, there was little disagreement.

At four-thirty on the afternoon of May 24, 1983, the jury was back in the courtroom. In the hush, Nash rose and, emotionless as always, faced his peers. Jury foreman Jean Shaw read the verdict. Guilty of murder in the second degree in the death of Margaret Barbera. Guilty of murder in the second degree in the death of Leo Kuranuki. Guilty of murder in the second degree of the death of Edward Benford. Guilty of murder in the second degree of the death of Robert Schulze. Guilty of conspiracy to commit the murder of Jenny Soo Chin.

Nash listened to the words, reacted not at all. He turned to Hochheiser, shook his hand, and said, "You did the best you could. Don't worry." He looked toward Waples, nodded, and smiled. He was led from the courtroom.

Thirty days later, on June 23, he was back in that same courtroom. Justice Scott looked down on him from the bench. What he had done, the justice said, "was a senseless waste of human life. I found nothing that mitigated the enormity of this man's crime." And then he passed sentence. For the murder of Margaret Barbera, twenty-five years to life. For the murder of Leo Kuranuki, twenty-five years to life. For the murder of Edward Benford, twenty-five years to life. For the murder of Robert Schulze, twenty-five years to life. The sentences were to run consecutively. For conspiracy to commit the murder of Jenny Soo Chin, eight and one half years to life, to run concurrently with the other sentences. He would have to serve one hundred years before he would be eligible for parole.

Much later, Richie Chartrand looked back and tried to figure it all out. "Donald," he said, "did all the things that a person should do for his wife and family. They never wanted for food. The bills were always paid. He found work, legal or illegal. He always found a way to make a buck. He was not abusive. He treated his wife's daughter, who was not his daughter, as if she was his own. Her child made his day and he did everything he could for that child just like any grandfather would do. But he decided to become a killer. Financially, he needed the money. And he figured out, well, hell, if they can do it, why can't I do it? Nowhere did we ever find anything that would indicate that he had ever done it before. But he sure as hell knew how to do it."

25

The shooter was gone, to the New York State penitentiary at Attica, to spend a hundred years in prison, never to see the outside world again as a free man. The man who had hired him, who had showed him the targets and had, in essence, supplied the bullets and aimed the weapon, remained in the limbo of the Metropolitan Correctional Center. How long he would remain there was a question. True, he had pleaded guilty to fraud and tax evasion. True, he had been sentenced to twenty-eight years. But that was the longest sentence for that kind of white-collar crime New York had ever seen, and there were many who thought that unless Irwin Margolies could be tried and convicted for his part in the murders, unless the evidence could be found to implicate him directly, an appeal would result in a sharp reduction of his sentence and he would soon walk the streets again, soon have in his grasp the millions he had done such deeds to attain.

But where was the evidence, and how was it to be obtained?

Donald Nash could supply it, of course. But he and Margolies were wrapped in a kind of unholy embrace. They had made a bargain of death and each would keep his part, for there was no gain to either in breaking it. Margolies had paid Nash for his work, had paid Nash's legal fees, was supporting Nash's family, and that was all that Nash wanted. So Nash would keep to his part and would say nothing. He had nothing to gain by talking. He was convicted and sentenced to spend the rest of his life in prison, and the authorities could offer him nothing in exchange for his testimony, could not and would not reduce that sentence, could not and would not send him back to the streets a free man.

If Margolies thought about it in the days following the end of the Nash trial, he must have been filled with growing confidence. He knew Nash would never talk. He was sure, too, of those others who knew what had happened and why. Would Madeleine Margolies turn on him? Unlikely. She was his wife. He had done much for her. He was doing all he could to protect and defend her in her misery. He would continue to do that, and he was sure he could count on her continued and undeviating loyalty. Would his brother-in-law, Scott Malen, talk? Unlikely. They were family, first of all, and families stuck together. Malen had already committed perjury before grand juries and had lied to prosecutors. If he changed his story, he could well be indicted for those lies, and the idea of prison did not sit well with that young man. And Malen was involved, certainly as an accessory after the fact. The implications of that ought to keep him silent.

Would friend and lawyer Henry Oestericher turn on him? Not likely. Oestericher was too deeply involved, had been part of the fraud scheme from its inception to its end, through all its twists and turns, had been part of the murders from the first moment such an idea came to Margolies. And Oestericher had lied repeatedly, to grand juries and authorities. Thus his career as an attorney, his welfare, his very freedom, Margolies was sure, depended on his maintaining his silence, on his maintaining the fictions.

214

Would Alberto Torres talk? He who had brought Nash and Margolies together, he who had seen Nash moments after the murders and knew about them? Unlikely—for he, too, had lied, and he was caught in those lies, and to tell the truth now would place him in danger, would brand him not only a perjurer but also an accessory after the fact to murder. Such a prospect, with its consequences, would not sit well with Torres, Margolies was convinced.

And there were no others. If Nash and Madeleine and Malen and Oestericher and Torres held to their silence and to their lies, Margolies had nothing to fear.

What Margolies did not count on was the willingness of the Manhattan district attorney to make deals to get him. For Waples and his superiors, for the cops, Margolies was the man they wanted, and they were willing to go to almost any lengths to get him. If that meant that Oestericher and Torres and Malen and anyone else, except Nash, went free, the price was worth paying if the end was Margolies where they thought he belonged.

"On the conclusion of Donald Nash's trial," Chartrand says, "we now go back and we touch base with everybody that we had spoken to before, everybody that had stonewalled us before. Their attitude has now changed. Alberto Torres now tells us exactly what happened on the night of the murders, what Donald told him he had just done, and now he tells us about the approach by Oestericher and the introduction of Donald Nash to Irwin Margolies at Ike and Mike's. And the only offering that he can give us as to why he had lied to us before was that he was afraid and that he really liked Donald, and in spite of his not telling us all of these things at that time, we still convicted Donald, so it didn't make any difference now. And, he said, he had trouble sleeping and looking at his wife and looking at his grandchildren. So now he bares his soul.

"Now, being aware of the introductions, of Nash and Oestericher and Margolies, we got back to Mr. Oestericher. And we make it quite clear, both through the New York district attorney and the federal prosecutor, that we are prepared to go ahead and include him in future indictments in the conspiracy to murder. We had talked to Mr. Oestericher many times before and he had always stonewalled us every time we brought him in. He's an attorney and he has a very glib tongue and he's a rather abrasive person. He talked to us to pacify us and then he'd say, 'Am I being charged or can I leave?' And we'd have to say, 'Good-bye, sir.' On one occasion, Augie Sanchez told him, 'You can leave, but probably the next time I meet you I will put you in custody.' And later on, Oestericher told us he had nightmares about Sanchez putting handcuffs on him. He was deathly afraid of Sanchez.

"But now that we have heard Torres, the situation has changed, and we explain that to Oestericher. He, the lawyer, now hires a lawyer, and it devastated him that he has to pay a lawyer because he doesn't have much, anyway. The lawyer agrees that it is in the best interest of justice if we can conclude a bargain and arrangements with his client so that Mr. Oestericher can freely tell us everything that he knows. And the arrangements are made and we conduct six consecutive Saturday interviews in his attorney's office and he tells us from the very beginning of the fraud case, and he tells us of his conversations with Alberto Torres, and he tells us of Torres's introduction of Donald to Irwin and the subsequent meetings of Irwin and Donald, and the conversations they held. He tells us many many things and we now have Irwin all wrapped up."

The bargain that was made with Oestericher was the classic one. He would be granted immunity from prosecution in exchange for his testimony. But, of course, there were a few other things that Oestericher had to agree to, as well, and the main one was an agreement to resign from the bar (had he not, he surely would have been disbarred). Similar bargains were struck with Torres and with Scott Malen.

With the decisions by Oestericher, Torres, and Malen that it was time for some truth-telling, and with the additional information provided by the government informants at the Metropolitan Correctional Center, Henry Adair and Vincent Calise, Waples went to a grand jury. On July 18, less than two months

216

after Nash's conviction, the jury handed down an indictment of Irwin Margolies on two counts of murder, for the killings of Margaret Barbera and Jenny Soo Chin, and one count of conspiracy to commit murder, that of David Blejwas. He was not indicted for the murders of the three CBS technicians since those were Nash's doing and Margolies had not hired him for that purpose even though he had later paid him a little extra because of that trouble.

Irwin Margolies was a very worried man that summer of 1983. His friends and allies had turned on him, and he could see little hope for his future. That was made increasingly clear to him during regular discussions at the district attorney's office. "The arrangements are made," Chartrand says, "that he will be brought out on occasions to the district attorney's office to see if he wants to sit there with his attorney and chat. Of course, he does not want to chat, but still we remove him for those little trips. And all of the court orders are made out in my name. And the arrangements are made with the feds that I will be the person that will remove him from time to time. And on each occasion, it's done by court order. And on the second visit there, I go up and I get Irwin one more time and now I bring him down and Richie Bohan is waiting for me and Irwin says, 'How are you, Mr. Bohan, how are you?' Because Irwin is very familiar with Bohan and very familiar with Augie Sanchez. But apparently he does not know who I am. He has seen me at his home and he has seen me in court, but he does not know who I am. He thinks perhaps I am an FBI agent, but he isn't sure. On this second trip down, Bohan says to me after we deliver him, 'You'll never believe this. He wants to know who the hell you are. He says he sees you all the time, you're always around, but he don't know who the hell you are.' I say, 'What the hell does he think? What did you say?' Bohan says, 'I said you're a detective, you're the guy that's going to arrest him.' Immediately thereafter, he knew who I was and he called me by name, Mr. Chartrand."

Those trips back and forth to the district attorney's office gave Margolies an idea. If everything looked decidedly grim,

217

then perhaps his one hope was escape. And then he heard rumors that an escape was actually being planned. In a nearby cell was a reputed organized-crime hit man named William Arico. Escape was one of Arico's penchants. He had, some time before, managed to get out of the prison on Rikers Island, get out of the country, and, with a contract from convicted Italian financier-swindler Michele Sindona, head for Italy, where he murdered officials investigating the collapse of the Sindona empire. On his return to the United States, he was recaptured and locked up in the Metropolitan Correctional Center while Italian authorities worked for his extradition on those murder charges. Arico was planning another escape.

When Margolies learned of the plan, he offered his help, financial and otherwise. The condition: When Arico was free, he was to intercept Margolies on one of those journeys between jail and the district attorney's office and set him free. Unfortunately for Arico and Margolies, as Arico was going out the window at the prison with another inmate, the bed sheet they were climbing down didn't hold. Arico fell. The other inmate fell on him. When the guards arrived, Arico was dead.

Word of Margolies's part in that aborted escape, and of his attempts to find somebody to replace Arico in his plans, got to Chartrand and other detectives. "We were extra cautious after that," Chartrand says. "And I let Irwin know that if there was a problem, he would be the first to hit the street."

The trial of Irwin Margolies opened in Supreme Court in Manhattan before Justice Eve Preminger on May 4, 1984. This time Gregory Waples did not move slowly to establish the crimes the defendant was charged with. He brought out his heaviest weapons right from the start. Henry Oestericher appeared on a witness stand, a broken man, no longer a lawyer, abandoned and disowned by his family, deeply in debt, a man in disgrace. He had a tale to tell: "I participated in the homicides of the CBS employees and the murders of Margaret Barbera and Jenny Soo Chin." In exchange for his testimony, "I was given full immunity."

218

He went through it all, the inception of the fraud, the talk of murder, the hiring of Nash, the murders themselves. He spared nothing, not even himself, while Margolies glared at him with unconcealed hatred.

He was followed by Alberto Torres, and there was his story of finding Nash, of introducing Nash to Margolies, and of Nash's revelations on the night of the killings.

There was the private detective, Linwood Lewis, who told of being hired to follow Barbera and get incriminating evidence against her; there was testimony about the phone calls between Nash and Margolies and Oestericher; there was testimony from David Blejwas about threats made against him by Margolies.

Scott Malen, with his grant of immunity, tied the knot even tighter around his brother-in-law as he told of paying Nash's lawyer his legal fees and of his own part in the frauds.

Waples even tried to win the testimony of Nash, but the convicted killer sat stonily on the stand and said he would plead the Fifth Amendment if asked any questions.

There was little Margolies's lawyer, Robert Hill Schwartz, could do to rebut the case against his client except to say, "The police and the FBI zeroed in on Irwin Margolies and paid any price to get him." It was not Margolies who was behind these "murders most foul," he declared. "The architect of all the murders . . . the foulest of a foul band of witnesses" was Henry Oestericher.

But the evidence, Waples countered, showed otherwise. If the witnesses against Margolies had been a foul band, nevertheless, he said, "sometimes you have to make a pact with the devil, so to speak, so you can get the mastermind."

It did not take the jury long. The six men and six women deliberated only a few hours and then marched back into the courtroom. Their only question, really, had been about the conspiracy to murder David Blejwas. Yes, there had been those tape recordings on which that plot had been discussed. Yes, there had been the testimony of Adair and Calise. But who could really believe such men? Who could find the guilt of anyone on their word? Of that charge, Margolies was acquitted.

But not so the others. The evidence had been overwhelming, conclusive. There were no doubts, reasonable or otherwise. Irwin Margolies was guilty of murder in the second degree in the murder of Margaret Barbera. Irwin Margolies was guilty of murder in the second degree in the murder of Jenny Soo Chin. Irwin Margolies was guilty of conspiracy to murder Margaret Barbera and Jenny Soo Chin.

On June 24, Margolies heard his future. Justice Eve Preminger, her scorn barely concealed, told him that he would spend fifty years of his life, if he had that many years, in New York State prison. She gave him twenty-five years to life on each count of murder, the terms to be served consecutively. And he would not begin serving them until he had finished the twenty-eight years he owed the U.S. government.

It was over. Irwin Margolies had reached for the gold ring on the merry-go-round of life and found it was only worthless brass. He had destroyed the lives of a dozen and more people, and had, in truth, taken the lives of five. He would have all the years of his future to consider what it was he had done and to contemplate the worth of his doing.

Long ago, the poet-philosopher Lao Tzu wrote:

> There is no calamity greater than lavish desires.
> There is no greater guilt than discontentment.
> And there is no greater disaster than greed.

HV
6534
N5
H35
1987
c.2

Hammer, Richard
    The CBS murders.